BORGES ON WRITING

BORGES ON WRITING

Edited by
Norman Thomas di Giovanni,
Daniel Halpern, and
Frank MacShane

E. P. Dutton & Co., Inc.
New York   1973

Published simultaneously in Canada

by Clarke, Irwin & Company Limited, Toronto and Vancouver

Library of Congress Catalog Card Number: 72-94692

SBN: 0-525-06997-6 (cloth)   0-525-47352-1 (paper)

Grateful acknowledgment is made for permission to reprint the following material:

"The End of the Duel." Reprinted by permission of E. P. Dutton & Co., Inc., from DOCTOR BRODIE'S REPORT, copyright © 1971, 1972 by Emecé Editores, S.A., and Norman Thomas di Giovanni. First appeared in *The New Yorker.*

Excerpts from "The Life of Tadeo Isidoro Cruz (1829–1874)." Reprinted by permission of E. P. Dutton & Co., Inc., from THE ALEPH AND OTHER STORIES 1933–1969, copyright © 1970 by Emecé Editores, S.A., and Norman Thomas di Giovanni.

"A Page to Commemorate Colonel Suárez, Victor at Junín." Reprinted by permission of Grove Press, Inc., from A PERSONAL ANTHOLOGY, copyright © 1967 by Grove Press, Inc.

"A Page to Commemorate Colonel Suárez, Victor at Junín" and "Conjectural Poem." Reprinted by permission of Delacorte Press/Seymour Lawrence from Jorge Luis Borges' SELECTED POEMS 1923–1967, copyright © 1968, 1969, 1972 by Emecé Editores, S.A., and Norman Thomas di Giovanni.

"June 1968," "The Keeper of the Books," "Invocation to Joyce," and "John 1:14." Reprinted by permission of *The New Yorker.* Copyright © 1969, 1972 by The New Yorker Magazine, Inc. These poems will appear in IN PRAISE OF DARKNESS, to be published in the Fall, 1973, by E. P. Dutton & Co., Inc.

"The Watcher." Reprinted by permission of *The New Yorker.* Copyright © 1972 by The New Yorker Magazine, Inc.

"The Writer's Apprenticeship" (entitled "Who Needs Poets?"). Reprinted by permission of *The New York Times.* Copyright © 1971 by The New York Times Company.

Portions of the main text first appeared in *Antaeus, The Columbia Forum,* and *Tri-Quarterly.*

Contents

3

Introduction

Many readers have been so interested in Borges' metaphysical complexities that they have forgotten he has had to face the same problem every writer faces—what to write about, what material to make use of. This is perhaps the fundamental task a writer must confront, for it will influence his style and mold his literary identity.

Borges has written on a wide range of subjects, but in his most recent work he has returned to his point of origin. The new stories in *The Aleph and Other Stories* and in *Doctor Brodie's Report* are based on his experiences as a young man living in the suburb of Palermo on the Northside of Buenos Aires. In a long autobiographical essay published in 1970, Borges described this part of the city as being made up "of low houses and vacant lots. I have often spoken of this area as a slum, but I do not quite mean that in the

American sense of the word. In Palermo lived shabby, genteel people as well as more undesirable sorts. There was also a Palermo of hoodlums, called *compadritos,* famed for their knife fights, but this Palermo was only later to capture my imagination, since we did our best—our successful best—to ignore it."

Here is the classic situation of the writer. Borges, the heir of a distinguished line of Argentine patriots, with English blood in his veins and military heroes as ancestors, found himself, through no fault of his own, living in a community on the skids where all the crudities of the New World were painfully obvious. In Palermo, the war between civilization and barbarism was fought every day.

For a while Borges kept Palermo out of his literary consciousness. And so almost every young writer shies away from writing about the life around him. He thinks it's dull or embarrassing. Father's a bore, mother a scold, the neighborhood is shabby and tedious. Who would be interested in it? Therefore the young writer often turns to an exotic subject and renders it in an exquisitely complex and obscure fashion.

To a degree, Borges did the same. Although he wrote some stories about Buenos Aires, for the most part he concentrated on literary subjects. "Life and death have been lacking in my life," he has said; he has also referred to himself as being "infested with literature." The results, in his early writing, were predictable. At a certain point he tried, he said, "to play the sedulous ape to two Spanish baroque seventeenth-century writers, Quevedo and Saavedra Fajardo, who stood in their own stiff, arid, Spanish way for the same kind of writing as Sir Thomas Browne in 'Urne-Buriall.'

I was doing my best to write Latin in Spanish, and the book collapses under the sheer weight of its involutions and sententious judgments." Then he tried another approach: he filled his work with as many Argentine expressions as he could find and, as he said, "worked in so many local words that many of my countrymen could hardly understand it."

And then, through some process that is mysterious and inexplicable, although certain evidence of maturity, Borges began to turn his attention to the life of suburban Palermo. After the mazes and the mirrors, the philosophical speculations concerning time and reality that occupied much of his early writing, he returned more and more to his own back yard, describing the process as "going back to sanity, to writing with some attempt at logic and at making things easy for the reader rather than dazzling him with purple passages." What helps make this important for us is that Borges' back yard is our back yard, for it is the modern city. Buenos Aires could be the prototype of the twentieth-century urban center, without history or character, no Inca or Aztec ruins, no Roman forum, no Acropolis. Like Los Angeles, Calcutta, São Paulo, or Sydney, it is an urban sprawl pleading for someone to give it expression.

But before he could deal with his own back yard, he had to sweep out the accumulated detritus. Mainly this meant that he had to deflate the romanticism of the gaucho, who was supposed to represent Argentine character. He had to go beyond the cheap reliance on local color that so much gaucho literature depended on. He did this by simple observation: the wide pampas became for him simply an "endless distance" where "the nearest house was a kind of blur on the horizon." As for the gauchos, they were just farmhands.

Once this preliminary work was done, once he revealed things as they were in the country, he was able to do the same thing for the city, and in the process become its spokesman. That is one reason for his universal appeal. His observations are always direct and clear, as a glance at a few sentences will tell. Here is the opening of "Rosendo's Tale," written only three years ago:

> It was about eleven o'clock at night; I had entered the old grocery store-bar (which today is just a plain bar) at the corner of Bolívar and Venezuela.

Note the authenticity: he does not say that the bar was in a remote or drab section of the city; no, it is on the corner of Bolívar and Venezuela, which is to say on the corner of Christopher Street and Seventh Avenue, or Wabash and Monroe. The world he gives you is a real one: it is not a sham, a bundle of half-digested myths or pieces of local color. Also, note the touch about the bar, which once was also partly a grocery store. This shows the author has been around long enough to know his subject. You can trust him.

With equal economy and competence he introduces a character:

> Benjamín Otálora, along about 1891, is a strapping young man of nineteen. He has a low forehead, candid blue eyes, and that country-boy appearance that goes with Basque ancestry.

Much of the quality of Argentine life is summarized here in a few words of physical description.

Borges' breakthrough has importance for readers and writers everywhere. He has shown people that they can face up to the experience of their lives. There is nothing to be ashamed of. Recently Borges has written: ["I have given up the surprises inherent in a baroque style as well as the surprises that lead to an unforeseen ending. I have, in short, preferred to satisfy an expectation rather than to provide a startling shock. For many years, I thought it might be given me to achieve a good page by means of variations and novelties; now, having passed seventy, I believe I have found my own voice."

Borges is a world writer because he knows all the rules and knows how and when to break them. His literary life has been a long struggle to liberate the word, to give it a new vitality in an age when it is constantly under attack. He is a magician of language, but like all the best tricksters and poets he makes us feel, when the trick is revealed and the poem said, that it was always there, somewhere unexpressed within us. Carlos Fuentes has written of Borges that without his prose, there would be no modern novel in South America today.

But Borges' influence has spread beyond the confines of Latin America: he has helped writers from all over the world. For this reason he was invited in the spring of 1971 to talk several times to the students enrolled in the graduate writing program at Columbia University. His blindness made it impossible for him to read the work of the students, but with the help of his colleague and trans-

9

lator, Norman Thomas di Giovanni, he was able to discuss his own work and therefore, by example, to help others in theirs. On each occasion, Borges and di Giovanni stayed for about two hours, and the audience, made up of students and faculty, was kept as small as possible so as to ensure a certain amount of intimacy.

To avoid needless repetition, it was decided that each of these meetings would be devoted primarily to a single topic: to the writing of fiction, of poetry, and of translation. Those present were provided with the text of one of Borges' stories, "The End of the Duel," with half a dozen poems, and with various samples of Borges' work translated by di Giovanni and others. For the fiction session, di Giovanni read the story line by line, and Borges interrupted when he wished to comment on it or discuss technical matters. Afterward, a general conversation took place, with Borges trying to explain how he gradually transformed his material into a story.

For the poetry meeting, the same method was followed, with di Giovanni reading the poems slowly and allowing for comments by Borges. During the question period, Borges discussed the usefulness of traditional forms of prosody and the need for knowing one's own literary heritage.

The translation seminar naturally involved di Giovanni more intimately as a participant, and he explained the way in which the two men worked together to put Borges' stories and poems into English. Each of the three occasions was informal. Borges' humor and modesty helped make these occasions congenial, as did di Giovanni's directness and unpretentiousness. The three meetings thereby provided the Columbia students and faculty the possibility of a close examination of a major writer's work, with the benefit of his own comments.

The text of this book is based on tape-recorded transcripts of the three meetings. Editing has been kept to a minimum in order to preserve the flavor of the actual occasions.

Following the last of his visits to the School of the Arts, Borges attended a reception held jointly for him and for the students and faculty of the writing program. There he spoke generally of the plight of the young writer, whether in Buenos Aires or New York, and these remarks are included in the appendix.

New York, June 1972

Part One
Fiction

Fiction

The fiction seminar was based on the text of Borges' story "The End of the Duel."

The End of the Duel

It's a good many years ago now that Carlos Reyles, the son of the Uruguayan novelist, told me the story one summer evening out in Adrogué. In my memory, after all this time, the long chronicle of a feud and its grim ending are mixed up with the medicinal smell of the eucalyptus trees and the babbling voices of birds.

We sat talking, as usual, of the tangled history of our two countries, Uruguay and the Argentine. Reyles said that probably I'd heard of Juan Patricio Nolan, who had won quite a reputation as a brave man, a practical joker, and a rogue. Lying, I answered yes. Though Nolan had died back in the nineties, people still thought of him as a friend. As always happens, however, he had his enemies as well. Reyles gave me an account of one of Nolan's many pranks. The thing had happened a short time before the battle of Manantiales; two gauchos from Cerro Largo, Manuel Cardoso and Carmen Silveira, were the leading characters.

How and why did they begin hating each other? How, after a century, can one unearth the long-forgotten story of two men whose only claim to being remembered is their last duel? A foreman of Reyles' father, whose name was Laderecha and "who had the whiskers of a tiger," had collected from oral accounts certain details that I transcribe now with a good deal of misgiving, since both forgetfulness and memory are apt to be inventive.

Manuel Cardoso and Carmen Silveira had a few acres of land that bordered each other. Like the roots of other passions, those of hatred are mysterious, but there was talk of a quarrel over some unbranded cattle or a free-for-all horse race in which Silveira, who was the stronger of the two, had run Cardoso's horse off the edge of the course. Months afterward, a long two-handed game of *truco* of thirty points was to take place in the local saloon. Following almost every hand, Silveira congratulated his opponent on his skill, but in the end left him without a cent. When he tucked his winnings away in his money belt, Silveira thanked Cardoso for the lesson he had been given. It was then, I believe, that they were at the point of having it out. The game had had its ups and downs. In those rough places and in that day, man squared off against man and steel against steel. But the onlookers, who were quite a few, separated them. A peculiar twist of the story is that Manuel Cardoso and Carmen Silveira must have run across each other out in the hills on more than one occasion at sundown or at dawn, but they never actually faced each other until the very end. Maybe their poor and monotonous lives held nothing else for them than their hatred, and that was why they nursed it. In the long run, without suspecting it, each of the two became a slave to the other.

I no longer know whether the events I am about to relate are effects or causes. Cardoso, less out of love than out of boredom, took up with a neighbor girl, La Serviliana. That was all Silveira had to find out, and, after his manner, he began courting her and brought her to his shack. A few months later, finding her in the way, he threw her out. Full of spite, the woman tried to seek shelter at Cardoso's. Cardoso spent one night with her, and by the next noon packed her off. He did not want the other man's leavings.

It was around that same time, just before or just after La Serviliana, that the incident of Silveira's sheepdog took place. Silveira was very fond of the animal, and had named him Treinta y Tres, after Uruguay's thirty-three founding fathers. When the dog was found dead in a ditch, Silveira was quick to suspect who had given it poison.

Sometime during the winter of 1870, a civil war broke out between the Colorados, or Reds, who were in power, and Aparicio's Blancos, or Whites. The revolution found Silveira and Cardoso in the same crossroads saloon where they had played their game of cards. A Brazilian half-breed, at the head of a detachment of gaucho militiamen, harangued all those present, telling them that the country needed them and that the government oppression was unbearable. He handed around white badges to mark them as Blancos, and at the end of his speech, which nobody understood, everyone in the place was rounded up. They were not allowed even to say goodbye to their families.

Manuel Cardoso and Carmen Silveira accepted their fate; a soldier's life was no harder than a gaucho's. Sleeping in the open on their sheepskin saddle blankets was something to which they were already hardened, and as for killing men, that held no difficulty for hands already in the habit of killing cattle. The clinking of stirrups and weapons is one of the things always heard when cavalry enter into action. The man who is not wounded at the outset thinks himself invulnerable. A lack of imagination freed Cardoso and Silveira from fear and from pity, although once in a while, heading a charge, fear brushed them. They were never homesick. The idea of patriotism was alien to them, and, in spite of the badges they wore on their hats, one party was to them the same as the other. During the course of marches and countermarches, they learned what a man could do with a spear, and they found out that being companions allowed them to go on being enemies. They fought shoulder to shoulder and, for all we know, did not exchange a single word.

It was in the sultry fall of 1871 that their end was to come. The fight, which would not last an hour, happened in a place whose name they never knew. (Such places are later named by historians.) On the eve of battle, Cardoso crept on all fours into his officer's tent and asked him sheepishly would he save him one of the Reds if the Whites won the next day, because up till then he had not cut anyone's throat and he wanted to know what it was like. His superior promised him that if he handled himself like a man he would be granted that favor.

The Whites outnumbered the enemy, but the Reds were better equipped and cut them down from the crown of a hill. After two unsuccessful charges that never reached the summit, the Whites' commanding officer, badly wounded, surrendered. On the very spot, at his own request, he was put to death by the knife.

The men laid down their arms. Captain Juan Patricio Nolan, who commanded the Reds, arranged the expected execution of the prisoners down to the last detail. He was from Cerro Largo himself, and knew all about the old rivalry between Silveira and Cardoso. He sent for the pair and told them, "I already know you two can't stand the sight of each other, and that for some time now you've been looking for a chance to have it out. I have good news for you. Before sundown, the two of you are going to have that chance to show who's the better man. I'm going to stand you up and have your throats cut, and then you'll run a race. God knows who'll win." The soldier who had brought them took them away.

It was not long before the news spread throughout the camp. Nolan had made up his mind that the race would close the proceedings, but the prisoners sent him a representative to tell him that they, too, wanted to be spectators and to place wagers on the outcome. Nolan, who was an understanding man, let himself be convinced. The bets were laid down—money, riding gear, spears, sabers, and horses. In due time they would be handed over to the widows and next of kin. The heat was unusual. So that no one would miss his siesta, things were delayed until four o'clock. Nolan, in the South American style, kept them waiting another hour. He was probably discussing the campaign with his officers, his aide shuttling in and out with the maté kettle.

Both sides of the dirt road in front of the tents were lined with prisoners, who, to make things easier, squatted on the ground with their hands tied behind their backs. A few of them relieved their feelings in a torrent of swearwords, one went over and over the beginning of the Lord's Prayer, almost all were stunned. Of course, they could not smoke. They no longer cared about the race now, but they all watched.

"They'll be cutting my throat on me, too," one of them said, showing his envy.

"Sure, but along with the mob," said his neighbor.

"Same as you," the first man snapped back.

With his saber, a sergeant drew a line in the dust across the road. Silveira's and Cardoso's wrists had been untied so that they could run freely. A space of some five yards was between them. Each man toed the mark. A couple of the officers asked the two not to let them down because everyone had placed great faith in them, and the sums they had bet on them came to quite a pile.

It fell to Silveira's lot to draw as executioner the mulatto Nolan, whose forefathers had no doubt been slaves of the captain's family and therefore bore his name. Cardoso drew the Red's official cutthroat, a man from Corrientes well along in years, who, to comfort a condemned man, would pat him on the shoulder and tell him, "Take heart, friend. Women go through far worse when they give birth."

Their torsos bent forward, the two eager men did not look at each other. Nolan gave the signal.

The mulatto, swelling with pride to be at the center of attention, overdid his job and opened a showy slash that ran from ear to ear; the man from Corrientes did his with a narrow slit. Spurts of blood gushed from the men's throats. They dashed forward a number of steps before tumbling face down. Cardoso, as he fell, stretched out his arms. Perhaps never aware of it, he had won.

DI GIOVANNI: All of you hold copies of "The End of the Duel" in your hands, but Borges has not heard the story since we translated it over a year ago. I'm going to begin reading the text so as to refresh his memory, and Borges is going to stop me now and then when he wants to comment.

"The End of the Duel": *It's a good many years ago now that Carlos Reyles, the son of the Uruguayan novelist, told me the story one summer evening out in Adrogué.*

BORGES: Well, this is a mere statement of what actually happened. I got the story from somebody else as well, but since it would have been awkward to mention two names and have two characters, I left out my other friend. Adrogué means a great deal to me because it stands for my boyhood and for my youth. It was the last place my father went to before he died, and I have very pleasant memories of it. Adrogué was once quite a fine little town, to the south of Buenos Aires, but now it has been spoiled by flats, garages, and television. But in its time it was full of *quintas,* with large gardens, and was a fine place to be lost in. Adrogué was a kind of maze, and there were no parallel streets. Reyles was the son of a famous Uruguayan novelist.

DI GIOVANNI: *In my memory, after all this time, the long chronicle of a feud and its grim ending are mixed up with the medicinal smell of the eucalyptus trees and the babbling voices of birds.*

BORGES: I don't think that calls for any comment; it's very obvious.

DI GIOVANNI: *We sat talking, as usual, of the tangled history of our two countries, Uruguay and the Argentine.*

BORGES: Yes, because the history of the República Oriental de Uruguay and our own history undoubtedly go together. In fact, my grandfather Borges was born in Montevideo. When he fought against Rosas in the battle of Caseros, he was, I think, fifteen or sixteen years old.

DI GIOVANNI: *Reyles said that probably I'd heard of Juan Patricio Nolan . . .*

BORGES: Yes, as a matter of fact I had . . . No, on the contrary, I made him up because I needed a third character for my story and, as all the other names are Brazilian or Spanish—and so as not to make the whole thing abound in local color—I made him into an Irishman, or into the son of an Irishman, Patricio Nolan. Patrick Nolan is Irish enough, I suppose.

DI GIOVANNI: *Reyles said that probably I'd heard of Juan Patricio Nolan, who had won quite a reputation as a brave man, a practical joker, and a rogue.*

BORGES: Here, in a sense, I'm being prophetic, because you'll soon find out what his jokes are like. Then, too, you're given the impression, I hope, of a rather grim country where the kind of story I'm going to tell is thought of as a joke.

DI GIOVANNI: *Lying, I answered yes. Though Nolan had died back in the nineties, people still thought of him as a friend. As always happens, however, he had his enemies as well. Reyles gave me an account of one of Nolan's many pranks.*

BORGES: He is calling it a prank in order to surprise you when you find out what that particular prank was—because it is more than a prank.

DI GIOVANNI: *The thing had happened a short time before the battle of Manantiales . . .*

BORGES: The battle of Manantiales stands for the revolution in Uruguay called *"La Guerra de Aparicio."*

DI GIOVANNI: *. . . two gauchos from Cerro Largo, Manuel Cardoso and Carmen Silveira . . .*

BORGES: Carmen is a woman's name, but it's fairly common for gauchos to have a woman's name if it doesn't end with an *a*. So a gaucho might be called Carmen Silveira. But since they are both rather ruthless characters, I thought it just as well one should have a man's name. Of course, their real names are forgotten, because they were all obscure gauchos.

DI GIOVANNI: *. . . Manuel Cardoso and Carmen Silveira, were the leading characters.*

BORGES: So there you have two Portuguese, or rather Brazilian, names. That kind of name is quite common in Uruguay and less so in the Argentine. I was also, at the same time, trying to get in local color and verisimilitude.

DI GIOVANNI: I want to ask you a question at this point. Was this a story that really happened? Did Carlos Reyles actually tell it to you?

BORGES: Yes, he told me the story, but I had to invent the circumstances and find names for the characters. He only spoke of "two gauchos," but that would have been too vague, so I gave them the names I thought proper—Cardoso and Silveira.

DI GIOVANNI: And Nolan you invented as a catalyst?

BORGES: As you've seen, I had to go in for some invention, but the story is a true one and I heard it twice over.

DI GIOVANNI: *How and why did they begin hating each other? How, after a century, can one unearth the long-forgotten story of two men whose only claim to being remembered is their last duel?*

BORGES: Here I'm playing an old literary trick—the trick of pretending I know nothing whatever about many things in order to make the reader believe in the others. In this case, however, it's true; I don't really know anything about the feud.

DI GIOVANNI: *A foreman of Reyles' father, whose name was Laderecha . . .*

BORGES: Such a foreman actually lived. Reyles told me about him and the name stuck with me because it was very strange. *"La derecha"* means "the right hand."

DI GIOVANNI: *. . . and "who had the whiskers of a tiger," . . .*

BORGES: That was also said by Reyles.

DI GIOVANNI: *. . . had collected from oral accounts certain details that I transcribe now with a good deal of misgiving, since both forgetfulness and memory are apt to be inventive.*

BORGES: This is true, I suppose. I allow myself to make these small observations now and then in order to avoid telling a bare or stark story.

DI GIOVANNI: That's what you and I always call the "trademark" when we're translating a story.

BORGES: Yes, I'm always repeating the same old tricks.

DI GIOVANNI: The second sentence of another story, "Pedro Salvadores," reads like this: "To meddle as little as possible in the telling, to abstain from picturesque details or personal conjectures is, it seems to me, the only way to do this."

BORGES: But I suppose other writers have other tricks, don't they?

DI GIOVANNI: Other trademarks.

BORGES: Yes, everybody has his own trademark—or someone else's for that matter, since we seem to be plagiarizing all the time.

DI GIOVANNI: *Manuel Cardoso and Carmen Silveira had a few acres of land that bordered each other. Like the roots of other passions, those of hatred are mysterious, but there was talk of a quarrel over some unbranded cattle or a free-for-all horse race in which Silveira, who was the stronger of the two, had run Cardoso's horse off the edge of the course.*

BORGES: That kind of thing is always happening, so here I wasn't inventing unlikely circumstances. For all I know, I was telling the truth. I had to account for the hatred between the two men—after all, that is the story—the fact of two gauchos hating each other in the solemn way they do. Gauchos are not talkative.

DI GIOVANNI: *Months afterward, a long two-handed game of* truco *of thirty points was to take place in the local saloon.*

BORGES: I don't suppose I could teach any of you *truco,* having no Spanish playing cards. Besides, I'm a poor hand at the game. But I got this right, I'm sure, since I've played it many times.

DI GIOVANNI: *Following almost every hand, Silveira congratulated his opponent on his skill, but in the end left him without a cent.*

BORGES: Personally, I saw that done in Buenos Aires between a *porteño*—a man from Buenos Aires—Nicolás Paredes, and somebody else who'd come from an inland province bordering on the Andes, La Rioja. Paredes kept congratulating the other man, saying that as a *porteño* he knew nothing whatever about the game and that he was getting a real lesson. Then at the end he won a hundred pesos or so and thanked him for them. I gave my gauchos that same trait. One gambler wins and pokes fun at the other by congratulating him. "Thank you, sir, for the lesson you've given me, and now I'm sorry to say I must accept your hundred pesos."

DI GIOVANNI: *When he tucked his winnings away in his money belt . . .*

BORGES: That is where gauchos keep their money—in a belt.

DI GIOVANNI: *. . . Silveira thanked Cardoso for the lesson he had been given. It was then, I believe, that they were at the point of having it out. The game had had its ups and downs. In those rough places and in that day, man squared off against man and steel against steel.*

BORGES: That even happened among *payadores*. Two men would be singing and playing their guitars in a contest, and one would suddenly walk out without a word. Then the first would leave and, finding the other lurking outside, they'd have it out with knives. They would go from one duel to another—from the guitar to the knife, their tools.

DI GIOVANNI: *But the onlookers, who were quite a few, separated them. A peculiar twist of the story is that Manuel Cardoso and Carmen Silveira must have run across each other out in the hills on more than one occasion at sundown or at dawn . . .*

BORGES: I had to invent that particular twist because, without it, how on earth could two men who were handy with their knives and who hated each other not have had it out? So I had to invent the circumstance and at the same time an explanation for it.

DI GIOVANNI: *. . . but they never actually faced each other until the very end. Maybe their poor and monotonous lives held nothing else for them than their hatred . . .*

BORGES: That was my own invention, as the White Knight had it.

DI GIOVANNI: *. . . and that was why they nursed it.*

BORGES: Yes. If you think of a gaucho or cowboy, you think of a romantic life, but these lives are not romantic for those who have to live them. They think of them as a day's work or, for all I know, a day's laziness.

DI GIOVANNI: *In the long run, without suspecting it, each of the two became a slave to the other.*

BORGES: Because when you hate somebody, you think about him all the time, and in that sense become his slave. The same thing happens when we fall in love.

DI GIOVANNI: *I no longer know whether the events I am about to relate are effects or causes. Cardoso, less out of love than out of boredom, took up with a neighbor girl, La Serviliana.*

BORGES: La Serviliana is not a common name except among the gauchos.

DI GIOVANNI: *That was all Silveira had to find out, and, after his manner, he began courting her and brought her to his shack. A few months later, finding her in the way, he threw her out.*

BORGES: That was common form.

DI GIOVANNI: *Full of spite, the woman tried to seek shelter at Cardoso's. Cardoso spent one night with her, and by the next noon packed her off.*

BORGES: He spent one night with her because he was a man, but after that he wanted none of her, since she had been his enemy's mistress.

DI GIOVANNI: *He did not want the other man's leavings.*

BORGES: One could quite understand that, I suppose.

DI GIOVANNI: *It was around that same time, just before or just after La Serviliana, that the incident of Silveira's sheep dog took place.*

BORGES: I had to invent the sheep dog and that incident, since the story had to be drawn out.

DI GIOVANNI: *Silveira was very fond of the animal, and had named him Treinta y Tres . . .*

BORGES: Treinta y Tres stands for the thirty-three heroes of Uruguay's history, who attempted to free their country from Brazilian rule, and succeeded. They crossed the River Uruguay to their native land, only thirty-three of them, and now Uruguay is an independent republic. I know many of their descendants.

DI GIOVANNI: *. . . after Uruguay's thirty-three founding fathers. When the dog was found dead in a ditch, Silveira was quick to suspect who had given it poison.*

Sometime during the winter of 1870, a civil war broke out between the Colorados, or Reds, who were in power, and Aparicio's Blancos, or Whites.

BORGES: These are the two traditional parties in Uruguay. The Colorados stood for what in Buenos Aires were called Unitarians; that is, they stood for civilization. The Blancos were not the gauchos—because the gauchos knew nothing whatever about politics—but, let's say, the rural population. *Blancos y Colorados.* Some of you who speak Spanish may know these two common phrases: *"Colorado como sangre de toro"*—red as a bull's blood; and *"Blanco como hueso de bagual"*—as white as the bones of a dead horse. They are still used in Uruguay.

DI GIOVANNI: *The revolution found Silveira and Cardoso in the same crossroads saloon where they had played their game of cards.*

BORGES: Since I had a saloon at my disposal, why not use it?

DI GIOVANNI: *A Brazilian half-breed, at the head of a detachment of gaucho militiamen, harangued all those present, telling them that the country needed them . . .*

BORGES: You see, he wasn't actually an *Oriental*, an Uruguayan; I made him a Brazilian because that would have been likely. The man himself should not be an Uruguayan, yet he should tell the Uruguayans about duty to country and so on. Also, Brazilians are fairly common in Uruguay.

DI GIOVANNI: . . . *telling them that the country needed them and that the government oppression was unbearable.*

BORGES: Of course, they know nothing whatever of government oppression in the country. All those things are beyond them; they are merely country folk, simple country folk.

DI GIOVANNI: *He handed around white badges to mark them as Blancos . . .*

BORGES: They knew nothing whatever about the whole thing. They were made into Blancos, but they might just as well have been made into Colorados. History, of course, was beyond them— and politics also. They didn't care a hang about any of it.

DI GIOVANNI: . . . *and at the end of his speech, which nobody understood, everyone in the place was rounded up. They were not allowed even to say goodbye to their families.*

BORGES: In *Martín Fierro,* our national poem—as people call it —Martín Fierro is permitted to say goodbye to his wife. Now in the story this isn't allowed, because the people would just have run away. So the Brazilian had them packed off and sent to the war.

DI GIOVANNI: *Manuel Cardoso and Carmen Silveira accepted their fate; a soldier's life was no harder than a gaucho's. Sleeping in the open on their sheepskin saddle blankets . . .*

BORGES: Yes, the *recado,* which was also used as pillows and blankets. It made a complicated kind of saddle: many rugs, or sheepskins, one on top of the other. In fact, what little I know of riding I learned on a *recado*.

DI GIOVANNI: . . . *was something to which they were already hardened, and as for killing men, that held no difficulty for hands already in the habit of killing cattle. The clinking of stirrups and weapons is one of the things always heard when cavalry enter into action.*

BORGES: I got that from my grandfather Acevedo. He was a civilian, but he had been in two or three battles, and he knew all about it. He told me that at first the men always felt afraid. I wonder whether you know those lines of Kipling, from a poem on the South African war: "He sees the blue white faces all trying hard to grin/ And then he feels his innards ailing and his bowels giving way," and so on. That's the kind of thing that happens, and then afterward you may be a hero.

DI GIOVANNI: *The man who is not wounded at the outset thinks himself invulnerable.*

BORGES: I was told this by a political boss in our Palermo neighborhood. He said that after the first shots were fired and you found out that you were not killed or wounded, you thought, well, this may go on forever.

DI GIOVANNI: *A lack of imagination freed Cardoso and Silveira from fear and from pity . . .*

BORGES: Here I should quote an English poet: "Cowards die many times before their deaths;/ The valiant never taste of death but once." My two gauchos have no imagination, however, so they were neither looking forward to battle nor fearing it.

DI GIOVANNI: *. . . although once in a while, heading a charge, fear brushed them.*

BORGES: Yes, because the fighting was all done by cavalrymen. There were no infantrymen in those civil wars. Everyone fought on horseback and used the lance and the spear.

DI GIOVANNI: *They were never homesick. The idea of patriotism was alien to them, and, in spite of the badges they wore on their hats, one party was to them the same as the other.*

BORGES: Naturally, politics was beyond them.

DI GIOVANNI: *During the course. of marches and countermarches, they learned what a man could do with a spear, and they found out that being companions allowed them to go on being enemies.*

BORGES: So that they could still have their private hatreds.

DI GIOVANNI: *They fought shoulder to shoulder and, for all we know, did not exchange a single word.*
   It was in the sultry fall of 1871 that their end was to come.

BORGES: As for the fall's being sultry, that had to be worked in for the sake of making it real. I wonder whether it really was sultry. But it generally is.

DI GIOVANNI: *The fight, which would not last an hour, happened in a place whose name they never knew.*

BORGES: That always happens in battles. Men were killed in the battle of Waterloo, but none of them had ever heard of the place.

DI GIOVANNI: *(Such places are later named by historians.) On the eve of battle, Cardoso crept on all fours into his officer's tent and asked him sheepishly would he save him one of the Reds if the Whites won the next day, because up till then he had not cut anyone's throat and he wanted to know what it was like.*

BORGES: This happened many times, because no quarter was given or asked for. Prisoners had their throats cut after a battle, and since that was expected, it came as no surprise to them. As for the man's creeping into his officer's tent, I know that kind of thing happened all the time. It was considered a kind of reward after battle to be allowed to cut somebody's throat.

DI GIOVANNI: *His superior promised him that if he handled himself like a man he would be granted that favor.*
The Whites outnumbered the enemy, but the Reds were better equipped and cut them down from the crown of a hill.

BORGES: That happened when my grandfather was killed. His rebel forces were far more in number, but the government forces —for the first time in Argentine history—had Remington rifles, and so the rebels were cut down. That was way back in 1874, some three or four years after this incident.

DI GIOVANNI: *After two unsuccessful charges that never reached the summit . . .*

BORGES: Since they only had spears and the others had rifles, they couldn't do anything and were killed off.

DI GIOVANNI: *. . . the Whites' commanding officer, badly wounded, surrendered. On the very spot, at his own request, he was put to death by the knife.*

BORGES: I think I can give you an anecdote, not of gauchos alone but of gauchos and Indians. There was a rather small fight on the western frontier of Buenos Aires, and the Pampas Indians were defeated. They knew that their throats were about to be cut, and their *cacique,* or chief, was badly wounded. Nevertheless, he managed to make his way toward the enemy—the government forces—and he said in broken Spanish, *"Mate, Capitanejo Payén sabe morir":* "Kill, Captain Payén knows how to die." Then he bared his throat to the knife, and it was duly cut.

DI GIOVANNI: *The men laid down their arms. Captain Juan Patricio Nolan, who commanded the Reds, arranged the expected execution of the prisoners down to the last detail. He was from Cerro Largo himself, and knew all about the old rivalry between Silveira and Cardoso.*

BORGES: Of course, I had to make him come from Cerro Largo; if not, he would not have heard about the two gauchos' being enemies of each other.

DI GIOVANNI: *He sent for the pair and told them, "I already know you two can't stand the sight of each other, and that for some time now you've been looking for a chance to have it out. I have good news for you.*

BORGES: Good news! He really meant it.

DI GIOVANNI: *Before sundown, the two of you are going to have that chance to show who's the better man. I'm going to stand you up and have your throats cut . . .*

BORGES: That would be called in Spanish *"degollar de parado."* It was rarely done, but I heard about it from my father.

DI GIOVANNI: *. . . and then you'll run a race. God knows who'll win." The soldier who had brought them took them away.*
It was not long before the news spread throughout the camp. Nolan had made up his mind that the race would close the proceedings, but the prisoners sent him a representative to tell him that they, too, wanted to be spectators and to place wagers on the outcome.

BORGES: They all felt curious, and they were very much interested in the race between the two doomed men.

DI GIOVANNI: *Nolan, who was an understanding man, let himself be convinced. The bets were laid down—money, riding gear, spears, sabers, and horses. In due time they would be handed over to the widows and next of kin. The heat was unusual. So that no one would miss his siesta, things were delayed until four o'clock.*

BORGES: These men, who were about to have their throats cut, wanted to get some sleep before the final sleep.

DI GIOVANNI: *Nolan, in the South American style, kept them waiting another hour.*

BORGES: That's always being done—in airports as well as military camps.

DI GIOVANNI: *He was probably discussing the campaign with his officers, his aide shuttling in and out with the maté kettle.*

BORGES: Maté is a kind of leisurely coffee we have.

DI GIOVANNI: *Both sides of the dirt road in front of the tents were lined with prisoners, who, to make things easier, squatted on the ground with their hands tied behind their backs.*

BORGES: Gauchos generally never sit down, except on cows' skulls. They just squat and find it comfortable.

DI GIOVANNI: *A few of them relieved their feelings in a torrent of swearwords, one went over and over the beginning of the Lord's Prayer, almost all were stunned. Of course, they could not smoke.*

BORGES: Naturally, because their hands were tied. That made it easier for the official cutthroat.

DI GIOVANNI: *They no longer cared about the race now, but they all watched.*

"They'll be cutting my throat on me, too," one of them said, showing his envy.

"Sure, but along with the mob," said his neighbor.

"Same as you," the first man snapped back.

BORGES: This is a rather ruthless story.

DI GIOVANNI: Gallows humor.

With his saber, a sergeant drew a line in the dust across the road. Silveira's and Cardoso's wrists had been untied so that they could run freely.

BORGES: So they wouldn't be hampered.

DI GIOVANNI: *A space of some five yards was between them. Each man toed the mark. A couple of the officers asked the two not to let them down because everyone had placed great faith in them, and the sums they had bet on them came to quite a pile.*

BORGES: This actually happened. Well, it was history, and pretty awful for them.

DI GIOVANNI: *It fell to Silveira's lot to draw as executioner the mulatto Nolan, whose forefathers had no doubt been slaves of the captain's family and therefore bore his name.*

BORGES: Slaves bore the names of their owners. I remember an old Negro who used to come to our house. Her name was Acevedo, which is my mother's name. Her family had been slaves of my grandparents, and she kept up the connection.

DI GIOVANNI: *Cardoso drew the Reds' official cutthroat, a man from Corrientes well along in years . . .*

BORGES: People from Corrientes and from Uruguay are supposed to be more ruthless. Gauchos from Buenos Aires hardly take to throat cutting, but the others have more Indian blood, and they seem to like that kind of thing—at least, they do it.

DI GIOVANNI: *. . . who, to comfort a condemned man, would pat him on the shoulder and tell him, "Take heart, friend. Women go through far worse when they give birth."*

BORGES: I heard that from my father, who got it from an old cutthroat: *"Ánimo, amigo; más sufren las mujeres cuando paren."*

DI GIOVANNI: *Their torsos bent forward, the two eager men did not look at each other. Nolan gave the signal.*
The mulatto, swelling with pride to be at the center of attention, overdid his job and opened a showy slash that ran from ear to ear . . .

BORGES: It was the first time he'd done it.

DI GIOVANNI: *. . . the man from Corrientes did his with a narrow slit.*

BORGES: Naturally, he knew a wide gash was not needed.

DI GIOVANNI: *Spurts of blood gushed from the men's throats. They dashed forward a number of steps before tumbling face down. Cardoso, as he fell, stretched out his arms. Perhaps never aware of it, he had won.*

BORGES: This is what always happens: we never know whether we are victors or whether we are defeated.

I'm afraid we've spent far too much time on details of local color and so on; I wonder whether any of you would like to talk in a more technical or literary way. I'm afraid I was enjoying the story and, strange as it may seem, forgot all about my duties as a lecturer or teacher. If you had objections to the story, that would be even better.

DI GIOVANNI: Borges, how long did you carry this story around in your head before you set it down?

BORGES: I must have carried it some twenty-five or thirty years. When I first heard it, I thought it was striking. The man who told it to me published it in *La Nación* under the title "Crepusculo rojo"—"Reddish Twilight"—but as he wrote it in a style full of purple patches, I felt I could hardly compete with him. After his death I wrote it down in as straightforward a way as possible. In between times, I carried it around in my memory for years, boring my friends with it.

DI GIOVANNI (*after some moments of silence*): You see, Borges, you've written such a perfect story that it calls for no comments or questions.

BORGES: Perhaps they're all fast asleep by now. (*To Frank Mac-Shane*) Why don't you say something? What are your chief objections to it?

MAC SHANE: My question about this story and others like it that are based on fact is how you expand particular details . . .

BORGES: What you're going to say is that I should have made those two characters quite different, but I don't think that two gauchos can be very different. They're just primitive folk. I couldn't have made them more complicated because that would have spoiled the story. They have to be more or less the same man.

DI GIOVANNI: But I don't think Frank was going to say that.

BORGES: Well, that was merely my guess, my fear, my hope.

MAC SHANE: I was interested in your use of the imagination on a subject like this.

BORGES: Some imagination has to be used. For example, I had to account for the fact of the two men's hating each other, and I had to give them names. It would have been awkward to go back and forth saying "the one" and "the other," or calling them "the first" and "the second." I made it easy by calling them "Cardoso" and "Silveira," both common Brazilian names.

MAC SHANE: In the end it doesn't come out as an anecdote but as a story. There's a difference between what you were told and what you wrote.

BORGES: I hope there's a difference. It's very hard to draw a line between story and anecdote; I have tried to make my piece sound true. That was my obvious duty as a storyteller. Do you think I should have written, "Two gauchos hated each other, and they were allowed to fight a duel after having their throats cut"? That would be too short and sweet, and also ineffective.

DI GIOVANNI: What Frank is getting at, Borges, is precisely the amount of imagination you poured in and the number of facts you left out. That is what makes it a story. Anyone here might have attempted a story with the facts you were given ...

BORGES: And made it far better than I did.

DI GIOVANNI: No doubt, no doubt.

BORGES: And you're all invited to do so, since the thing actually happened and it doesn't belong to me.

DI GIOVANNI: But can you say something about how you sift the material and take only what you want? For instance, can you remember any facts that you didn't use from the anecdote you were told?

BORGES: No, because I was told it in a very bare way, and then Reyles wrote it down in a way full of purple patches and fine writing—the kind of thing I do my best to avoid. I can't write like that; I only went in for what might be called circumstantial invention. For example, I had to make them play *truco,* and I invented the episode about the sheep dog, and I gave him the right name—Treinta y Tres—because that's the kind of name a dog might have, although they are generally called Jazmín.

MAC SHANE: Do you sometimes take one factual episode and combine it with another to make something new—a new story from two completely disconnected and different sources?

BORGES: Yes. In this story, for example, I witnessed the *truco* game not in Uruguay, but in the old Northside of Buenos Aires.

QUESTION: I wonder whether Señor Borges would tell us what he means by a primitive character?

BORGES: I wonder what I mean myself. That they were just simple country folk, I suppose; that they don't analyze their feelings. They don't think of a battle before it happens, because you need imagination for that. Men who live in the present do not look forward to their fates, and that's hinted at a good many times in the story. They are taken to the war, but they don't know what the war's about; they care nothing about it. And when they are given a chance to have a good long nap before having their throats cut, they go to sleep. The other prisoners are rather curious about the duel; they want to see it. They don't mind waiting these five minutes or so before their own throats are cut. Some are afraid, since one of them attempts the Lord's Prayer, though he can't find his way to the end because he doesn't know the words.

QUESTION: Does selectivity mean that fiction has to be less unlikely than life?

BORGES: Yes, because as Boileau said, *"La réalité n'est pas toujours vraisemblable."* Reality is not always probable, or likely. But if you're writing a story, you have to make it as plausible as you can, because otherwise the reader's imagination will reject it.

DI GIOVANNI: I know this is a great concern of yours because you're always telling me, "This is the way it actually happened, but I can't use it because it sounds so unlikely." You're always toning things down.

BORGES: I suppose every writer has to do that, because if you tell an improbable story in an improbable way, it's utterly hopeless.

QUESTION: A characteristic I've found in this story and in others you've written is that you always suggest there are other factors, other truths besides the ones you relate. I was wondering whether there is anything you can finally establish as being true and as having existence—aside from yourself?

BORGES: I wouldn't even include myself. I think one should work into a story the idea of not being sure of all things, because that's the way reality is. If you state a given fact and then say that you know nothing whatever of some second element, that makes the first fact a real one, because it gives the whole a wider existence.

QUESTION: I believe that in one of your essays you wrote that a short story can be centered either on the characters or on the situation. In this story, characterization is at a minimum . . .

BORGES: It had to be minimal because the two characters are more or less the same character. They are two gauchos, but they could be two hundred or two thousand. They are not Hamlets or Raskol-nikovs or Lord Jims. They are just gauchos.

QUESTION: Then the situation is what counts?

BORGES: Yes, in this case. And generally speaking, what I think is most important in a short story is the plot or situation, while in a novel what's important are the characters. You may think of *Don Quixote* as being written with incidents, but what is really important are the two characters, Don Quixote and Sancho Panza. In the Sherlock Holmes saga, also, what is really important is the friendship between a very intelligent man and a rather dumb fellow like Dr. Watson. Therefore—if I may be allowed a sweeping statement—in writing a novel, you should know all about the characters, and any plot will do, while in a short story it is the situation that counts. That would be true for Henry James, for example, or for Chesterton.

QUESTION: Do you find some special vision of life in the anecdotes you use?

BORGES: I find that most of my stories come from anecdotes, although I distort or change them. Some, of course, come from characters, from people I know. In the short story, I think an anecdote may serve as a beginning point.

QUESTION: Do you think the changes you make are inherent in the anecdote?

BORGES: Well, that's a hard nut to crack. I don't know if they're inherent in the anecdote or not, but I know that I need them. If I

46

told a story swiftly and curtly, it wouldn't be effective at all. I have
tried to make this one effective by slowing it down. I couldn't begin by saying, "Two gauchos hated each other," because nobody
would believe it. I had to make the hatred seem real.

QUESTION: When did you write "The End of the Duel"?

BORGES: I must have written it a year ago. No. Yes. (*To di Giovanni*) You know far more about it than I do, because you know
something about dates and I don't.

DI GIOVANNI: About fourteen months ago.

BORGES: Good for you. I accept this plausible invention of yours.

QUESTION: I'd like to know what it was in the anecdote about the
two gauchos that fascinated and obsessed you for thirty years.

BORGES: That's a very difficult question. I don't know—you might
as well ask me why I like coffee or tea or water.

QUESTION: Was it the joke of it?

BORGES: No, not the joke. I thought of it as being a grim story, and
I made it into a joke to make it still more grim. I invented some
people telling the story in a comic way in order to make it harder
and more pitiless.

DI GIOVANNI: But the story itself is the answer to what he saw in
the anecdote, isn't it?

BORGES: It should be, but perhaps I failed and then it needs another answer or a postscriptum. Personally, do you find the story too trivial or too flat?

QUESTION: No, I find it horrifying.

BORGES: Well, it's meant to be horrifying or what we used to call hard-boiled, and in order to make it horrifying I left the horror to the reader's imagination. I couldn't very well say, "What an awful thing happened," or "This story is very gruesome," because I would make a fool of myself. That kind of thing must be left to readers, not to writers. Otherwise, the whole thing goes to pieces.

DI GIOVANNI: The story is much more gruesome to us than it is to Borges or anyone else in the Argentine.

BORGES: No! I'm not so ruthless.

DI GIOVANNI: I know, but what I mean is that this is practically a tradition with you. Cutting throats is something Argentines are familiar with.

QUESTION: It's not the bloodiness; it's the fact that two men lived their lives to die.

DI GIOVANNI: Well, how do they differ from the rest of us in that?

BORGES: Something else might be added which I didn't add because I thought it was implied by the story. The two men were grateful for this chance they were provided in death—the one

48

chance in their lives—to find out, after their years of hating each other, who was the better man. This was their duel.

QUESTION: But is that what appealed to you?

BORGES: Perhaps.

QUESTION: That's what I wanted to hear you say.

BORGES: In that case, you are revealing something to me that is really true—here in New York and not in Buenos Aires, where I wrote the story. What appealed to me was the fact that the two men did not think of themselves as victims. They were given the chance of their lives.

DI GIOVANNI: There is something else that hasn't come out here. Borges wrote this story immediately after an earlier one called "The Duel," which was a completely different kind of story.

BORGES: A very quiet Henry James kind of story.

DI GIOVANNI: This later one comes as a sharp contrast and was called in the original "El otro duelo"—"The Other Duel," or "Another Duel." We couldn't use that title in English when publishing the story separately in *The New Yorker,* since it only makes sense alongside "The Duel."

BORGES: That other story is about two society ladies who are close friends and rivals. After this almost Jane Austen kind of story, we get this bit of gruesome realism from the Banda Oriental of Uruguay.

DI GIOVANNI: The ladies are painters, and they're painting against each other.

QUESTION: It seems to me there's a strong element in common between "The End of the Duel" and "The South." They both seem to have the same senseless bitterness. Would you care to comment on that?

BORGES: I would hardly agree with you because "The South" is really a story of wishful thinking. When I think of my grandfather who died in action, when I think of my great-grandfather who had to fight his kinsmen in the wars of the dictator Rosas, when I think of people in my family who had their throats cut or who were shot, I realize I'm leading a very tame kind of life. But really I'm not, because after all they may have just lived through these things and not felt them, whereas I'm living a very secluded life and am feeling them, which is another way of living them—and perhaps a deeper one, for all I know. In any case, I shouldn't complain of being a man of letters. There are harder destinies than that, I suppose.

But in "The South," the real plot is about—well, actually there are several plots. One of them might be that the man died on the operating table, and that the whole thing was a dream of his, in which he was striving to get the death he wanted. I mean, he wanted to die with a knife in his hand on the pampa; he wanted to die fighting as his forefathers had fought before him. But in "The End of the Duel" I don't think there was any such wishful thinking. In fact, I wouldn't want to have been one of the two gauchos. I think I would have funked it—I wouldn't have run the race, I'd have fallen on my face.

QUESTION: I heard you say you weren't much interested in time in this story, but in a strange way the two fight their duel after they're dead, when they've gone beyond time.

BORGES: That's a good observation, and it shows that I can't get rid of my obsession with time.

QUESTION: What do you think about the idea that fiction must be engaged in the political and social issues of the times?

BORGES: I think it is engaged all the time. We don't have to worry about that. Being contemporaries, we have to write in the style and mode of our times. If I write a story—even about the man in the moon—it would be an Argentine story, because I'm an Argentine; and it would fall back on Western civilization because that's the civilization I belong to. I don't think we have to be conscious about it. Let's take Flaubert's novel *Salammbô* as an example. He called it a Carthaginian novel, but anyone can see that it was written by a nineteenth-century French realist. I don't suppose a real Carthaginian would make anything out of it; for all I know, he might consider it a bad joke. I don't think you should try to be loyal to your century or your opinions, because you are being loyal to them all the time. You have a certain voice, a certain kind of face, a certain way of writing, and you can't run away from them even if you want to. So why bother to be modern or contemporary, since you can't be anything else?

MAC SHANE: I think the questioner also had in mind political and social issues. Do you think they should be dealt with in fiction?

BORGES: In this story, there was nothing of the kind.

DI GIOVANNI: But there is.

BORGES: There may have been, for all I know, but I wasn't concerned about that. I was concerned with the idea of the two men running a race with their throats cut and of the whole thing's being thought of as a joke or prank. Naturally, this story is wound up with the history of Argentina and of Uruguay and of the gauchos. It has associations with the whole of South American history, the wars of liberation, and so on. But I wasn't concerned about that. I was merely trying to tell my story in a convincing way. That was all I was concerned about, although you can link it to anything you like.

DI GIOVANNI: And in spite of your aims, it's a hell of a statement about politics at that time and in that place. It should satisfy anybody.

BORGES: And perhaps it's about the politics of any time or any place, I don't know. Of course, these politics are a bit picturesque.

QUESTION: How do you think the artist should relate to his own time?

BORGES: Oscar Wilde said that modernity of treatment and subject should be carefully avoided by the modern artist. Of course, he was being witty, but what he was saying was based on an obvious truth. Homer, for example, wrote several centuries after the Trojan war. The idea that a writer should be contemporaneous is itself modern, but I should say it belongs more to journalism than to literature. No real writer ever tried to be contemporary.

QUESTION: You quote from many sources in your writings, from many languages all over the world. One question I have—I hope it isn't rude—is whether these are real or invented quotations.

BORGES: Some of them, I'm sorry to say, are real. But not all of them. In the present story, however—"The End of the Duel"—I have done my best to be as straightforward as I can. I got the trick out of Kipling's *Plain Tales from the Hills,* his first work. I am now giving up erudition, or sham erudition. I try to write simple, straightforward stories.

QUESTION: There is a story about an encyclopedia . . .

BORGES: I suppose you are referring to "Tlön, Uqbar, Orbis Tertius," in which the whole world is being changed by the encyclopedia. I wrote that story when I was quite a young man. I wouldn't attempt that kind of thing today—after all, I want to change. I want to try my hand at being somebody else, at writing in a different way, in an unexpected way.

QUESTION: In one of your stories you say we might be characters in another person's dreams.

BORGES: Yes, that story is "The Circular Ruins," and for all we know it may be true. You are dreaming me. No, I'm wrong. I am dreaming you.

QUESTION: How does this idea of dream work?

BORGES: It's a very ancient idea, an idea of the idealists, of Berkeley and the Hindus, and also of the Red King in Lewis Carroll, I think.

QUESTION: How did you ever dream up Pierre Menard, the author of the *Quixote?*

BORGES: I had undergone an operation, and I didn't know whether I could go on writing. Then I said to myself, if I attempt a short critical essay and fail, then I'll know there's no hope left for me. If I'd attempted a poem, that wouldn't have told me anything, because the spoils are given by the muse or the Holy Ghost. So I attempted something new—a story which was also a bit of a hoax—and when I got away with that I saw I could go back to literature and be, well, not a happy man, because nobody is happy, but at least I could feel that my life was in some way justified. Many people in Buenos Aires and two literary men of my acquaintance took the whole thing seriously. One of them said to me, "Of course, I know all about Pierre Menard. I suppose he was out of his mind." And I said, "Yes, I suppose so, but it was an interesting kind of madness, wasn't it?" It was one of the first stories I ever wrote. I keep saying it was the first story, but in fact it was the second or third.

QUESTION: How do you know when an anecdote may be useful to you?

BORGES: When I hear an anecdote that I think is interesting, I tell it to my friends. Then, somehow, I feel that I should write it down. This happens years and years afterward. If you tell me an anecdote today, it wouldn't find its way into print until some four or five years from now, because the process is a slow one. I suppose other writers may hear an anecdote and the story is given them at once, but in my case I have to sit back and wait, and then, when the moment comes, I have to be very receptive and try not to tamper or tinker with it.

QUESTION: I'd like to ask something about your story "Street-corner Man."

BORGES: That was the first story I ever wrote. I dislike it heartily.

QUESTION: It's been said that it was influenced by the gangster films of Josef von Sternberg.

BORGES: Yes, it was, and also by Chesterton's stories. I attempted that story as a literary experiment. I wanted to write a story in which all things would be visual. So that story wasn't written in a realistic mode at all. I thought of the whole thing as a kind of ballet. Later on, I rewrote the story as it might have happened and called it "Rosendo's Tale." When I wrote "Streetcorner Man," I knew quite well it was all unreal, but as I wasn't striving after reality I didn't mind. I just wanted to write a very vivid and visual story. It came out in a rather operatic way, and I must apologize to you for that.

QUESTION: In the Sternberg films there is a balance between the visual and the realistic. How much of that did you have in mind?

BORGES: I was thinking of Josef von Sternberg and of Chesterton all the time. I am most thankful to Sternberg because he achieved his ends very effectively, but whereas he was attempting a film and had to be visual, in my case I think visual effects weren't really needed. You can tell a story without being too vivid or visual. In fact, I think if you are too vivid you're really creating unreality, because the fact of seeing things in that way blurs them. I knew that my story was unreal, but I never thought that people would take it at face value. In the foreword to the book it appeared in, *A Universal History of Infamy,* I even mentioned Stevenson, Chesterton, and those admirable films of Sternberg.

QUESTION: It's a beautiful story, though.

BORGES: I venture to disagree with you. It's the worst thing I ever wrote.

DI GIOVANNI: Everybody in Buenos Aires loves the story . . .

BORGES: Because it's sentimental, because it provides the reader with the illusion that once we were very brave and very daring and very romantic.

QUESTION: But it's become something important in Latin American literature. I think it has a new approach.

DI GIOVANNI: The point is that Borges never wrote anything like it again. He went on to do much better things. "Streetcorner Man" was written in 1933.

BORGES: Of course, many people think I have fallen off since that story.

DI GIOVANNI: His new book, *Doctor Brodie's Report,* goes back to the same themes, but in a completely different way.

BORGES: Yes, in a straightforward way.

DI GIOVANNI: The characters in that story were standing on a stage and shouting at the audience. It helps being an Italian to appreciate it because it's so operatic.

QUESTION: In many of your stories and poems you seem concerned with time.

BORGES: Well, time as given by the watch is conventional, isn't it? But real time, for example, when you're having a tooth pulled, is only too real. Or quite different, say, from the time of fear, when the sands of time run out. Yes, I have always been obsessed by time.

QUESTION: We've had questions about the writer and his responsibility to his time and questions about reality and dreams. There's a line in "Pedro Salvadores," and I wonder whether it explains your point of view.

BORGES: If I could remember the line it would help me.

QUESTION: It says, ". . . he had no particular thoughts, not even of his hatred or his danger. He was simply there—in the cellar. . . ."

BORGES: I thought of Pedro Salvadores as a simple-minded man. I wonder if it might interest you to know that I met his grandson two months ago. He has the same name as Salvadores, and he set me right by telling me that his grandfather had spent twelve years in the cellar, not nine as I had written, and that he was a military man. That latter fact would have done me no good, because I wouldn't expect a soldier to be hiding in a cellar for twelve years, whereas a civilian might be allowed that. Besides, Salvadores didn't know he had to wait that long. Maybe he thought every night would be the last one.

DI GIOVANNI: I don't know if that answers the question. Does it?

BORGES: No, perhaps not. But I've forgotten all about the beginning of the question.

QUESTION: In your story "The Aleph" you have a character named Borges. Since I presume what happens to him is fiction and not truth, I wonder why you use your own name.

BORGES: Well, I thought of that kind of thing happening to myself. Besides, I'd been jilted by Beatriz Viterbo—of course, under another name—and so I used my own name.

DI GIOVANNI: Which you've done in several places.

BORGES: Yes, I always do it; of course, I don't try to make myself into a laughing butt. It's an old literary trick—the kind of thing Boswell did when he wrote Johnson's life. He made himself into a ridiculous character, but he wasn't. Boswell was a very intelligent man.

Now I think I heard a question—or perhaps I've been hearing it so often I imagined I heard it this particular time—about a writer's duty to his time. I think a writer's duty is to be a writer, and if he can be a good writer, he is doing his duty. Besides, I think of my own opinions as being superficial. For example, I am a conservative, I hate the Communists, I hate the Nazis, I hate the anti-Semites, and so on; but I don't allow these opinions to find their way into my writings—except, of course, when I was greatly elated over the Six Days' War. Generally speaking, I think of keeping them in watertight compartments. Everybody knows my opinions, but as for my dreams and my stories, they should be allowed their full freedom, I think. I don't want to intrude into them, I'm writing fiction, not fables.

Perhaps I should be more clear. I am an antagonist of *littérature engagée* because I think it stands on the hypothesis that a writer can't write what he wants to. To illustrate, let me say—if I may be autobiographical—I don't choose my own subjects, they choose me. I do my best to oppose them, but they keep on worrying me and nagging me, and so I finally have to sit down and write them and then publish them to get rid of them.

One must also remember that there is often a difference between what a writer means to do and what he actually does. I am now thinking of an *écrivain engagé,* Rudyard Kipling, who was trying to remind his absentminded British countrymen that they had somehow managed to collect an Empire, and of course he was thought of as something of a foreigner for saying that sort of thing. In the end he wrote a book called (and here we have British understatement) *Something of Myself*—not everything, but only a little bit of himself—and at the end he says that a writer must be allowed to write against his own private moral position. He cites as an example the great Irish writer Swift, who was indignant against mankind, but who also, in the first part of *Gulliver's Travels,* wrote something that is a delight to children.

QUESTION: I wonder whether you would comment on your opposition to the Perón regime.

BORGES: Yes, why not? My opposition was public, but it didn't find its way into my literary output. I was giving my lectures all the time; I was president of the Argentine Society of Writers, and at every lecture I got in my dig at Perón. Everybody knew I was against him, and the proof of that is that as soon as we got our *Revolución Libertadora,* I was made Director of the National Library. They needed an anti-Peronista, and they knew about me. My mother, my sister, and my nephew had all been in prison; I was hounded by a detective who, by the way, was anti-Perón but who had to do his job. But I never blended any of that into my stories or poems. I kept them apart, so that I think I was a good Argentine and at the same time I did my best to be a good writer, not mixing the two things together.

QUESTION: What about the story you did about the Nazi lieutenant?

BORGES: "Deutsches Requiem." What happened in that story is quite different. I, of course, was on the Allied side—the American side. When the Germans were defeated I felt a great joy and relief, but at the same time I thought of the German defeat as being somehow tragic, because here we had perhaps the most educated people in Europe, who have a fine literature, a fine tradition of philosophy and of poetry. Yet these people were bamboozled by a madman named Adolf Hitler, and I think there is tragedy here. Then I tried to imagine what a real Nazi might be like—I mean someone who really thought of violence as being praiseworthy for its own sake. Then I thought this archetype of the Nazis wouldn't mind being defeated; after all, defeats and victories are mere matters of chance. He would still be glad of the fact, even if the Americans and English won the war. Naturally, when I am with Nazis, I find they are not my idea of what a Nazi is, but this wasn't meant as a political tract. It was meant to stand for the fact that there was something tragic in the fate of a real Nazi. Except that I wonder if a real Nazi ever existed. At least, when I went to Germany, I never met one. They were all feeling sorry for themselves and wanted me to feel sorry for them as well. They were very sentimental and rather sloppy.

QUESTION: I'm told that at one time you published an anthology of detective stories. Would you tell us about that?

BORGES: I suppose the choices I made were fairly obvious. I began with the "onlie begetter," Edgar Allan Poe, and then I found different stories—for instance, "The Big Bow Mystery" by Israel

Zangwill, a fine story by Jack London, and then obvious examples from Chesterton, Eden Phillpotts, Ellery Queen, and so on. But I think of Poe as the man who invented the whole genre. All detective stories come from him, although Wilkie Collins tried his hand at it in a very different way. He wrote long detective novels in which the characters are more important than the plot—except in *The Moonstone,* where the plot is very fine.

QUESTION: And Conan Doyle?

BORGES: Yes, I remember that I translated one of his best stories, "The Redheaded League." This work was all done with a fine Argentine writer, Adolfo Bioy-Casares. We went over everything very carefully, and we very carefully left out Dorothy Sayers because we didn't like her stuff.

MAC SHANE: Would you care to say something about your collaboration with Bioy-Casares and how it differs from your own work?

BORGES: It's different because when we are together, as the Greeks might have put it, there's a third man. That is, we do not think of ourselves as two friends or even two writers; we just try to evolve a story. When somebody asks me, "Did that sentence come from your side of the table or the other?" I can't tell him. And I don't know which of us invented the plot. That's the only way it can be done. But why should we talk of Bioy-Casares, since here I have at my elbow Norman Thomas di Giovanni? We work in the same spirit. When we attempt a translation, or a re-creation, of my poems or prose in English, we don't think of ourselves as being two men.

We think we are really one mind at work. I suppose that's what Plato did in his dialogues. When he had many characters, he wanted to see many sides of the question. Perhaps the only way of arriving at a collaboration is that way—of two or three men thinking of themselves as being one man, of forgetting personal circumstances and yielding themselves completely to the work and to its perfection.

QUESTION: At the end of your essay "New Refutation of Time," you wonder whether you'll be able to work out a new ethical system. Have you?

BORGES: No, I don't think so. Besides, the title is meant as an irony. If time doesn't exist, you can't make a new refutation of it. But when I called it "Nueva refutación del tiempo" I was having a kind of joke on myself. I believe in the argument logically, and I think that if you accept the premises, the argument may stand—though at the same time, alas, time also stands. And that's far sounder than any reasoning of mine, or even of Hume, Berkeley, or Schopenhauer.

QUESTION: I'd like to know why you've left the world of the fantastic and of the encyclopedia and come closer to a real world.

BORGES: I've done that because there are quite a few literary hands in Buenos Aires who are writing Borges' stories for me. They are going in for mazes and mirrors, for tigers and so on, and of course they do it far better than I can. They are younger men, whereas I'm rather old and tired. Besides, I want to try my hand at new things; this latest volume of mine, *Doctor Brodie's Report,* which may seem tame to many readers, is in a sense a venture, an experiment for me.

QUESTION: You've talked very informatively about the difference between short stories and novels. Have you ever been impelled to write a novel?

BORGES: No, because I've hardly ever felt impelled to read a novel. I'm fond of short stories, but I'm far too lazy for novel writing. I'd get tired of the whole thing after writing ten or fifteen pages. But, in fact, I recently wrote a long short story called "El Congreso"— "The Congress"— which may be one of my best stories. At least, I think it is because it's the latest story I've written, and you need that kind of feeling in order to go on writing.

QUESTION: I think of these stories about duels as being stylized forms of encounters between two people, and this entails that they be contemporaneous. Yet in your "New Refutation of Time" you say there are no contemporaneous moments. I don't see how you reconcile this.

BORGES: I don't see it either, sir. I agree with you.

QUESTION: If they can't be contemporaneous, they'd have to be immortal.

BORGES: In that case, you have to write that story because it is your invention, not mine. I think it would be a quite different one, and quite fine.

QUESTION: I believe you have said that when writers achieve fame it is for the wrong reason. Do you think that is true of yourself?

BORGES: I'm quite sure of it. I believe people think kindly of me in this country firstly because kindness seems to come easily to them, but also because they think of me as a foreigner, and a foreigner can hardly be a rival. They also think of me as being totally blind, and blindness calls for sympathy. So you see, these elements —being a foreigner, being an old man, and being blind—make for a very strong combination.

DI GIOVANNI: Of course, your fame has nothing to do with anyone's having read your stories.

BORGES: People are fond of me in spite of my stories, I should say.

QUESTION: When you write a story like "Pierre Menard," are you playing a joke on other people, or on yourself?

BORGES: I think I'm playing an impersonal joke. I'm not fooling anybody. I'm not fooling myself. I'm doing it for the sheer fun of it.

DI GIOVANNI: I'm afraid our time is up.

BORGES: But, of course, as time is unreal. . . .

Part Two
Poetry

Poetry

MAC SHANE: I think the simplest way to begin is to ask Borges to make some general comments about the writing of his own poetry.

BORGES: Yes, why not? Of course, one of the tricks is not to lecture. Whatever happens will have happened—things belong to the past quite quickly. Well, I think I'll start the ball rolling by making some very platitudinous and obvious remarks on the subject. After all, we are all trying to be poets. In spite of my failures, I still keep trying to be a poet. (At any moment I will be seventy-two years old.)

I think young poets are apt to begin with what is really the most difficult—free verse. This is a very great mistake. I'll fall back on what the Argentine poet Leopoldo Lugones said way back in 1909 in a book that is still revolutionary—*Lunario senti-*

mental. In the foreword, he wrote that he was attempting experiments in verse—that he was trying his hand at the invention of new meters and at new combinations of the "old-time" meters, such as eight-syllable verse, eleven-syllable verse, fourteen-syllable verse, and so on. He knew that what he was attempting was rash and very probably a failure, but he wanted to remind his readers that he had already demonstrated that he could handle the classical forms of verse. He added that one can't start by being a revolutionary, but that in his case he felt that he had already earned the right to experiment, since he had published several volumes of good poetry, or at least tolerable classic verse. I think this is an honest statement, but it is merely an ethical argument. A better argument could be found, if necessary. If you attempt a sonnet, for example, you believe in the illusion that you really have something before you, and that is the framework of the sonnet, whether you choose the Italian form or the Shakespearean form. This form exists before you've written a single line of verse. Then you have to find rhyming words. These rhyming words limit what you are doing and make things easier for you. Now this does not mean that I prefer a sonnet to a piece of free verse. I like both. If you take some of the best pages in Walt Whitman's *Leaves of Grass* and ask me whether or not I find them better than a sonnet by Shakespeare or Wordsworth or Keats or Yeats, I would say that the question is meaningless. There is no need to like one and discard the other, since you can keep both. But the difference is this: if you attempt a sonnet, you already have something given to you, and the reader can anticipate the form, while if you attempt free verse, everything must come from within you. You have to be far more skillful technically to attempt free verse than to attempt what you may think of as being old-fashioned. Of course, if you happen to be Walt Whitman, you'll have the inner strength, or inner urge, that makes you capable and worthy of free verse, but this doesn't happen to many of us. I committed that mistake when I published my first volume, *Fervor de Buenos Aires,* way back in 1923. I wrote that book in free verse—I had read my Whitman, of course—because I thought it was easier. Now I know that it is far more difficult. If I have to write something on the spur of the moment, if I have to construct something in a hurry, I fall back on a set form, because it's easier for me. So, my advice to young poets is to begin with the classical forms of verse and only after that become revolutionary. I remember an observation by Oscar Wilde—a prophetic observation. He said, "Were it not for the sonnet, the set forms of verse, we should all be at the mercy of genius." This is what's happening today; at least this is what's happening in my country. Almost every day I receive books of verse that put me at the mercy of genius—that is to say, books that seem to me quite meaningless. Even the metaphors in them are not discernible. Metaphor supposedly links two things, but in these books I see no links whatever. I get the impression that the whole thing has been done in a haphazard way, as though by a crazy computer of some kind. And I am expected to feel or enjoy something! I committed that mistake of genius in my first book (I think in my second book also; perhaps even in my third), and then I discovered that there is something really magical and unexplainable about the sonnet. This form, which in itself seems to be half haphazard with its various patterns and rhyme schemes—Italian, Shakespearean, Spenserian —is capable of producing very different kinds of poems.

What I'm saying is that, in the long run, to break the rules, you must know *about* the rules. Now all this is very obvious, but in spite of its being obvious, it doesn't seem to be understood by most young people, let alone elderly ones, as in my case. In a moment we can go into some of my verses, which, proving that I'm not very sure of what I have been saying, will be, I fear, in free verse. But I have returned to free verse after trying other verse forms.

This leads me to another interesting subject: why do I sometimes write in free verse and sometimes write sonnets? This is a kind of central mystery—how my poems get written. I may be walking down the street, or up and down the staircase of the National Library—I'm thinking now of Buenos Aires—and suddenly I know that something is about to happen. Then I sit back. I have to be attentive to what is about to happen. It may be a story, or it may be a poem, either in free verse or in some form. The important thing at this point is not to tamper. We must, lest we be ambitious, let the Holy Ghost, or the Muse, or the subconscious—if you prefer modern mythology—have its way with us. Then, in due time, if I have not been bamboozling myself, I am given a line, or maybe some hazy notion—a glimpse perhaps—of a poem, a long way off. Often, I can barely make it out; then that dim shape, that dim cloud, falls into shape, and I hear my inner voice saying something. From the rhythm of what I first hear, I know whether or not I am on the brink of committing a poem, be it in the sonnet form or in free verse. This is one way of doing it.

The other way, which I don't think is as good, is to have a plot beforehand. That plot, however, is also "given" to me. For example, two or three days ago I suddenly found that I had an idea for the plot of a poem. But it's still too early for me to do anything with it—it has to bide its time, and in due course it will follow. Once I've committed myself to two or three lines, I know the general shape of the whole thing, and I know whether it will be in free verse or in some conventional form. All this boils down to a simple statement: poetry is given to the poet. I don't think a poet can sit down at will and write. If he does, nothing worthwhile can come of it. I do my best to resist this temptation. I often wonder how I've come to write several volumes of verse! But I let the poems insist, and sometimes they are very tenacious and stubborn, and they have their way with me. It is then that I think, "If I don't write this down, it will keep on pushing and worrying me; the best thing to do is to write it down." Once it's down, I take the advice of Horace, and I lay it aside for a week or ten days. And then, of course, I find that I have made many glaring mistakes, so I go over them. After three or four tries, I find that I can't do it any better and that any more variations may damage it. It is then that I publish it. Now, why do I publish it? Alfonso Reyes, the great Mexican prose writer, and sometimes the greatest Mexican poet, told me, "We have to publish what we write, because if we don't, we keep on changing it, trying all the possible variations, and we don't go beyond that."

73

So the best thing is to publish it and go on to other things. I know very little of my own work by heart, because I don't like what I write. In fact, I find myself personally expressed far better in the writings of other poets than in my own, because I know all my mistakes—I know all the chinks and all the padding, I know that a particular line is weak, and so on. I read other poets in a different way; I don't look too closely at them. And now, before we read a poem of mine, are there any questions? I am most thankful for questions, and I might add that I don't like agreement. I like being set right.

QUESTION: As for writing in set forms, don't you think it depends on the kind of poetry you grew up on? For example, I can't imagine writing sonnets or rhyming couplets.

BORGES: I am very sorry. But I think it is rather strange that you should be so little curious about the past. If you are writing in English, you are following a tradition. The language itself is a tradition. Why not follow that long and illustrious tradition of sonnet writers, for example? I find it very strange to ignore form. After all, there are not many poets who write good free verse, but there are many writers who have mastered the other forms. Even Cummings wrote many fine sonnets—I know some of them by heart. I don't think you can possibly discard all of the past. If you do, you run the risk of discovering things that have already been discovered. This comes from a lack of curiosity. Aren't you *curious* about the past? Aren't you curious about your fellow poets in this century? And in the last century? And in the eighteenth century?

Doesn't John Donne mean anything to you? Or Milton? I can't really even begin to answer your question.

QUESTION: One can read the poets of the past and interpret what is learned into free verse.

BORGES: What I fail to understand is why you should *begin* by attempting something that is so difficult, such as free verse.

QUESTION: But I don't find it difficult.

BORGES: Well, I don't know your writing, so I can't really say. It might be that it is easy to write and difficult to read. In most cases, I think it has something to do with laziness. There are, of course, exceptions—such as Whitman, Sandburg, Edgar Lee Masters. I think one argument for free verse is that the reader knows he is not expected to get any information out of it or to be argued into believing something—unlike a page of prose, which might belong to what De Quincey called the literature of knowledge and not to the literature of power. The reader expects to get emotion out of free verse—to feel elevated and quickened into life, to feel torn by emotions. What I mean is, in free verse there is something that is going to affect him physically. Even if it's not very musical, and it generally isn't, the reader still knows the spirit the poet wants him to have when he's reading the poem.

QUESTION: I think it's difficult to relate to forms that are old and often unfamiliar. Do you think it is possible to create new forms to write in?

BORGES: Well, I suppose that theoretically it might be possible. But what I really wanted to say, and I haven't said it yet, is that there is always a structure, and that it's easier to begin with an obvious structure. There *has* to be structure. I thnk Mallarmé said, "There is no such thing as prose; the moment you care about rhythm, it becomes verse." This would go with what Stevenson said: "The difference between verse and prose lies in the fact that when you are reading"—he meant the classical forms of verse— "you expect something, and you get it." But he also said of prose that a sentence has to end in an unexpected and yet pleasing way, and this is often quite difficult. On the other hand, Monsieur Jourdain said that he spent his life speaking in prose without knowing it. He was mistaken. One doesn't speak in prose, one tries to make oneself understood. If I wished to write down what I said, I would be attempting prose, and I would have different problems to solve.

All this, in a nutshell, means that the difference between, let's say, a sonnet by Keats and a page of free verse by Whitman lies in the fact that in the case of the sonnet the structure is obvious—and so it is easier to do—while if you try to write something like "Children of Adam" or "Song of Myself," you have to invent your own structure. Without structure, the poem would be shapeless, and I don't think it can afford to be that. So, let's do a poem now. Perhaps we should begin with "June 1968." It is autobiographical—or at least I thought it was. I was feeling happy when I wrote the poem, but maybe I wasn't feeling as happy as I thought. My friend Norman Thomas di Giovanni will read his translation of the poem, and we can stop to discuss it at different points.

June 1968

On a golden evening,
or in a quietness whose symbol
might be a golden evening,
a man sets up his books
on the waiting shelves,
feeling the parchment and leather and cloth
and the satisfaction given by
the anticipation of a habit
and the establishment of order.
Stevenson and that other Scotsman, Andrew Lang,
will here pick up again, in a magic way,
the leisurely conversation broken off
by oceans and by death,
and Alfonso Reyes surely will be pleased
to share space close to Virgil.
(To arrange a library is to practice,
in a quiet and modest way,
the art of criticism.)
The man, who is blind,
knows that he can no longer read
the handsome volumes he handles
and that they will not help him write
the book which in the end might justify him,
but on this evening that perhaps is golden
he smiles at his strange fate

and feels that special happiness
which comes from things we know and love.

DI GIOVANNI: "June 1968"
On a golden evening,
or in a quietness whose symbol
might be a golden evening . . .

BORGES: The whole point of the poem is that strange happiness I
felt, although I was blind, of going back to my own books and
putting them on the shelves. I thought myself quite clever when I
did so. The fact that the man (who is me) is blind is hinted at
throughout the poem.

DI GIOVANNI: I might remind you that this event took place just
after you had come back from a year at Harvard, and you were
setting up a new apartment. Returning to your books after a long
absence was that much more pleasurable.

BORGES: Naturally, I was just back in my home town. I was
touching those books again. I was feeling them, although I could
no longer read them.

DI GIOVANNI: *On a golden evening,*
or in a quietness whose symbol
might be a golden evening . . .

BORGES: This is where blindness is hinted at. I do not know
whether the evening was golden, because I couldn't see it. I'm
hinting at the blindness. Happiness and blindness are the central
subjects of the poem. You see, it is "in a quietness whose symbol

might be a golden evening." For all I knew, it could have been dismal weather.

DI GIOVANNI: . . . *a man sets up his books*
on the waiting shelves,
feeling the parchment and leather and
cloth . . .

BORGES: There again you get the suggestion that the man is blind. But you don't get it in too obvious a way. Nothing is said about the texts of the books or the lettering. He is enjoying the books, not with his eyes but with his fingers.

DI GIOVANNI: . . . *and the satisfaction given by*
the anticipation of a habit
and the establishment of order.

BORGES: When I was putting those books on the shelves, I knew that I would remember where I had put them, and so that day stood for many happy days to come. Also involved here is the idea that this was just a beginning, that what I was doing today would go on and administer to a possible or even probable future.

DI GIOVANNI: *Stevenson and that other Scotsman, Andrew*
Lang . . .

BORGES: They are favorites of mine, and friends.

DI GIOVANNI: . . . *will here pick up again, in a magic way,*
the leisurely conversation broken off
by oceans and by death . . .

BORGES: Because Stevenson died before Andrew Lang. Andrew Lang wrote a very fine article about him in a book called *Adventures Among Books*. They were fast friends, and I suppose they had many fine literary conversations together. These are two men whom I love personally, as if I had known them. If I had to draw up a list of friends, I would include not only my personal friends, my physical friends, but I would also include Stevenson and Andrew Lang. Although they might not approve of my stuff, I think they would like the idea of being liked for their work by a mere South American, divided from them by time and space.

DI GIOVANNI: *. . . and Alfonso Reyes surely will be pleased to share space close to Virgil.*

BORGES: I have mentioned Alfonso Reyes because he was one of the finest friends I had. As a young man in Buenos Aires, when I was no one in particular except Leonorcita Acevedo's son or Colonel Borges' grandson, Reyes somehow divined that I would be a poet. Remember, he was quite famous. He had renewed Spanish prose and was a very fine writer. I remember I used to send him my manuscripts, and he would read not what lay in the manuscript itself but what I had intended to do. Then he would tell people what a fine poem this young man Borges had written. But on looking into the poem, and not having his magic power, they would see nothing in it but my mere clumsy attempts at versification. Reyes, I don't know how, read what I had intended to do and what my literary clumsiness had prevented me from doing.

Virgil is brought in because, for me, he *stands* for poetry. Chesterton, who was a very witty and a very wise man, said of someone who had been accused of imitating Virgil that a debt to Virgil is like a debt to nature. It is not a case of plagiarism. Virgil is here for all times. If we take a line from Virgil we might as well say that we took a line from the moon or the sky or the trees. And, of course, I knew that Reyes, in his own secret heaven, would be pleased to find himself near Virgil. Anyway, I think of arranging books in a library—in a mild and modest way—as a kind of literary criticism.

DI GIOVANNI: Those are the next three lines, Borges.

> . . . (*To arrange a library is to practice,*
> *in a quiet and modest way,*
> *the art of criticism.*)

BORGES: Yes, I am quite incapable of invention. I must fall back on that minor South American writer, Borges.

DI GIOVANNI: *The man, who is blind . . .*

BORGES: Now you see the fact that the man is blind. We might call that the key phrase, the central fact—the idea of happiness in blindness. I say it in an offhand way. I don't say the man *is* blind, because that would be a kind of sweeping statement; it would be too affirmative. But "The man, who, by the way, is blind," makes it more effective, I think. It's a different voice; you have to throw the information in by the way.

DI GIOVANNI: *. . . knows that he can no longer read*
the handsome volumes he handles
and that they will not help him write
the book which in the end might justify
him . . .

BORGES: At that time, I had many plans for writing books. I hoped I would be able to write a book on Old English poetry, and perhaps a novel or a book of stories. At the same time, I doubted whether I could actually do so. In any case, those books made for something friendly—a kind of friendly encouragement.

DI GIOVANNI: But you have written two books since this poem.

BORGES: Well, I am sorry. I must apologize. I can't avoid writing —it's a bad habit! I have an anecdote which I can tell, since, after all, I'm not talking to all of you but to each of you—in confidence. I remember I was once talking to an old flame of mine. She had been the most beautiful woman in Buenos Aires. I had been in love with her, but she had always rejected me. The first time she ever saw me, she made a gesture which meant "No! Don't propose marriage to me. No!" But after all that was over, we had a kind of stock joke between us. I once said to her, "Well, we've known each other for such a long time, and here we are. . . ." I was about to be sentimental. Then she said to me (she was Irish-Norwegian), "No, I'm just a bad habit." And I have that bad habit of writing. I can't stop myself.

DI GIOVANNI: *. . . but on this evening that perhaps is golden . . .*

BORGES: Another reminder of his blindness.

DI GIOVANNI: *. . . he smiles at his strange fate*
and feels that special happiness . . .

BORGES: Because being blind and also getting pleasure from the possession of books is a strange fate. Besides, I was also setting up a new home, and I was looking forward to different forms of happiness.

DI GIOVANNI: *. . . which comes from things we know and love.*

BORGES: This poem is altogether autobiographical. The thought came to me that something else might be tried, based on that same experience. But when I tried it for the second time, I said, "I'll be more inventive and forget all about myself; I'll write some kind of fairy story or a parable—perhaps after Kafka." I was very ambitious—perhaps I still am! Anyway, I finally ended up writing a sham Chinese poem. You can see it is Chinese because of the many details. But, in fact, the poem is a kind of transformation. It's the same experience as "June 1968," transmogrified. Maybe to the casual reader the two poems are not the same. But I know they are the same—on my word of honor.

The Keeper of the Books

Here they stand: gardens and temples and the reason
    for temples;
exact music and exact words;
the sixty-four hexagrams;

ceremonies, which are the only wisdom
that the Firmament accords to men;
the conduct of that emperor
whose perfect rule was reflected in the world,
      which mirrored him,
so that rivers held their banks
and fields gave up their fruit;
the wounded unicorn that's glimpsed again,
      marking an era's close;
the secret and eternal laws;
the harmony of the world.
These things or their memory are here in books
that I watch over in my tower.

On small shaggy horses,
the Mongols swept down from the North
destroying the armies
ordered by the Son of Heaven to punish their desecrations.
They cut throats and sent up pyramids of fire,
slaughtering the wicked and the just,
slaughtering the slave chained to his master's door,
using the women and casting them off.
And on to the South they rode,
innocent as animals of prey,
cruel as knives.
In the faltering dawn
my father's father saved the books.
Here they are in this tower where I lie

calling back days that belonged to others,
distant days, the days of the past.

In my eyes there are no days. The shelves
stand very high, beyond the reach of my years,
and leagues of dust and sleep surround the tower.
Why go on deluding myself?
The truth is that I never learned to read,
but it comforts me to think
that what's imaginary and what's past are the same
to a man whose life is nearly over,
who looks out from his tower on what once was city
and now turns back to wilderness.
Who can keep me from dreaming that there was a time
when I deciphered wisdom
and lettered characters with a careful hand?
My name is Hsiang. I am the keeper of the books—
these books which are perhaps the last,
for we know nothing of the Son of Heaven
or of the Empire's fate.
Here on these high shelves they stand,
at the same time near and far,
secret and visible, like the stars.
Here they stand—gardens, temples.

DI GIOVANNI: "The Keeper of the Books"
Here they stand: gardens and temples and the
reason for temples . . .

85

BORGES: You see, gardens and temples make you think of something heathen and ancient.

DI GIOVANNI: . . . *exact music and exact words;*
the sixty-four hexagrams . . .

BORGES: I was thinking of the *Book of Changes,* or the *I Ching,* and the sixty-four hexagrams, which are six lines each.

DI GIOVANNI: . . . *ceremonies, which are the only wisdom*
that the Firmament accords to men . . .

BORGES: There I was doing my best to be Chinese. You have hexagrams, ceremonies, and a firmament. I was trying to be as Chinese as a good student of Arthur Waley should be.

DI GIOVANNI: . . . *the conduct of that emperor*
whose perfect rule was reflected in the world,
which mirrored him . . .

BORGES: That's cribbed from Confucius—in translation, of course.

DI GIOVANNI: . . . *so that rivers held their banks*
and fields gave up their fruit;
the wounded unicorn that's glimpsed
again . . .

BORGES: That refers to some biography or legend of Confucius. It seems that when his mother was about to give birth to him, a unicorn appeared (I saw a picture of that unicorn), and a river started from the horn. Time passed, and the unicorn came back, and Confucius then knew that his life was over. We are also reminded of Mark Twain and Halley's Comet. These are two wonderful things that appear and disappear at the same time—the unicorn and Confucius, the comet and Mark Twain.

DI GIOVANNI: *. . . marking an era's close . . .*

BORGES: "Marking an era's close" may be too contemporary. At my time of life one is apt to think that the country's going to the dogs. As a matter of fact, the country is always going to the dogs, and is always saved—somehow.

DI GIOVANNI: *. . . the secret and eternal laws;*
the harmony of the world.

BORGES: That is being Chinese and prophetic, I suppose.

DI GIOVANNI: *These things or their memory are here in books*
that I watch over in my tower.

BORGES: I am going back disguised as a Chinese to my first poem here.

DI GIOVANNI: *On small shaggy horses,*
the Mongols swept down from the North . . .

BORGES: The horses had to be small, because if I had said "On high shaggy horses" it would have been too grandiose. I keep them ponies, to be on the safe side.

DI GIOVANNI: *. . . destroying the armies*
ordered by the Son of Heaven to punish their
desecrations.

BORGES: Here I was trying to make the reader feel sorry for the Son of Heaven, who sends armies to punish these Mongols but is defeated instead.

DI GIOVANNI: *They cut throats . . .*

BORGES: I have to apologize to all of you for the throat cutting. I was merely being an Argentine—it's a habit we have. In fact, one of my forefathers had his throat cut. It was done very deftly and very quickly. I think it's far better than the hot seat!

DI GIOVANNI: *They cut throats and sent up pyramids of fire,*
slaughtering the wicked and the just,
slaughtering the slave chained to his master's
door . . .

BORGES: It seems that that was a habit in Eastern nations. There is something in Chuang Tzu about a porter's being chained to a door. And then in Flaubert's *Salammbô,* when Hannibal walks in to see his treasures, there is also a chained slave.

DI GIOVANNI: *. . . using the women and casting them off.*
And on to the South they rode,
innocent as animals of prey,
cruel as knives.

BORGES: Yes, I think of them as wolves rather than men.

DI GIOVANNI: *In the faltering dawn*
my father's father saved the books.

> *Here they are in this tower where I lie*
> *calling back days that belonged to others,*
> *distant days, the days of the past.*

BORGES: It would have to be a tower, because it would probably remain standing after the rest of the village had been destroyed. From the tower he could see many things. And now I come to the fact that he can't see.

DI GIOVANNI: *In my eyes there are no days. The shelves . . .*

BORGES: You see, he's been lying all the time.

DI GIOVANNI: *. . . stand very high, beyond the reach of my years,*
                       and leagues of dust and sleep surround the
                       tower.

BORGES: Originally, I wrote that line, *"leguas de polvo y sueño,"* at Alicia Jurado's *estancia*. She later used it as a title for a book.

DI GIOVANNI: *Why go on deluding myself?*
                    The truth is that I never learned to read,
                    but it comforts me to think
                    that what's imaginary and what's past are the
                    same . . .

BORGES: I am—to be very old-fashioned—piling on the agonies. I speak of the man as being blind, as having lost the power of reading the books, and then I go on to something worse—to the fact that he is illiterate and that he has never been able to read. His fate, in a sense, was, or is—I don't know which word I should use, since all this is imaginary—worse than mine. I, at least, had read Stevenson, but he couldn't read his books of wisdom.

DI GIOVANNI: . . . *that what's imaginary and what's past are the same*
> *to a man whose life is nearly over,*
> *who looks out from his tower on what once was city*
> *and now turns back to wilderness.*

BORGES: He knew this, though he hadn't actually seen it.

DI GIOVANNI: *Who can keep me from dreaming that there was a time*
> *when I deciphered wisdom*
> *and lettered characters with a careful hand?*
> *My name is Hsiang. . . .*

BORGES: I got the name from Chuang Tzu, but I have no idea how it's pronounced.

DI GIOVANNI: . . . *I am the keeper of the books—*
> *these books which are perhaps the last,*
> *for we know nothing of the Son of Heaven*
> *or of the Empire's fate.*

BORGES: Here again is the idea of civilization going to pot.

DI GIOVANNI: *Here on these high shelves they stand,*
> *at the same time near and far,*
> *secret and visible, like the stars.*

BORGES: Again, I am talking about the secret presence of the books that you get in the first poem. This second poem might be thought of as a kind of fable or parable, but I'm still writing from my personal experience.

DI GIOVANNI: And the closing line:
Here they stand—gardens, temples.

BORGES: To my great surprise, I think this is quite a good poem—even though I wrote it. I wonder what you think of it.

QUESTION: Can he still see gardens and temples from inside the tower?

BORGES: No, he can't. The whole town has been destroyed. The idea is that within the books a lost order is still to be found—civilization. I think of civilization, in this poem, as having been destroyed by the Mongols. And yet, that order—that Asian civilization where the whole thing happened, let's say, a century or more ago—is still there in the books, only nobody can decipher them, because this man is the only one alive, and he is blind.

QUESTION: Do you think it is possible to write major poetry in more than one language?

BORGES: I wonder whether it has been done. I think it's very difficult to write major poetry in a single language, yet perhaps there were people who could do that kind of thing in the Middle Ages—with Latin, for example. We can look into the case of Eliot. I'm not sure if he's a major poet, but I am quite sure that his French poems are quite bad. I can remember another case—Rubén Darío, who had a very fine and sensitive knowledge of French. When he attempted French versification the result was beneath contempt. George Moore thought he was a good French scholar; I don't think he was, and his French verses are nowhere. They are a kind of joke. Milton was a great English poet, but I think of what he wrote in Italian as a kind of exercise.

QUESTION: I wonder if you have anything to say about the influence of surrealism on the younger poets in America.

BORGES: I know very little about surrealism, but I was a great reader of the German expressionists, who came before them. I attempted Spanish translations of poets such as Wilhelm Klemm, Johannes Becher, and August Stramm—those men who wrote in *Der Aktion*. But, of course, it couldn't be done. The beauty of those poems depended on compound words, and you can't do that kind of thing in Spanish. The result was a miserable failure. The same sort of thing happens in translating Joyce. But to get back to the question, I suppose that when you speak of surrealism you are thinking about a kind of poetry beyond reality. Are you aware that attempts at that were made before the surrealists, and some of them are far better? *Alice in Wonderland* and *Through the Looking-Glass* are examples. There are also lines in Yeats. In one of his poems he speaks of "That dolphin-torn, that gong-tormented sea." He is not thinking of any sea of geography or of the imagination or even of dreamland. He often creates a new object, and that—if it works out—is legitimate. From a theoretical point of view, all experiments should be tried and anything is possible. My first remarks merely concern the fact that perhaps it is easier to use the usual forms than to try and invent new ones; and that, in any case, it is safer to know all about them instead of starting out by breaking the rules. Every young poet thinks of himself as Adam, naming things. The truth is that he is not Adam and that he has a long tradition behind him. That tradition is the language he is writing in and the literature he has read. I think it is wiser for a young writer to delay invention and boldness for a time and to try merely to write like some good writer he admires. Stevenson said that he began by playing the "sedulous ape" to Hazlitt. Of course, the phrase "sedulous ape" is proof of Stevenson's originality. I don't think Hazlitt would have used the expression "sedulous ape."

DI GIOVANNI: Borges, do you want to say something about how you actually write the poems? The poems we just read are originally dictated in Spanish. How much do you think a poem out in your head before you begin dictating? What do you sound out?

BORGES: Naturally, I try them on myself. I read in Kipling's *Something of Myself* that he tried out every line and that when he had purified them of mistakes, he would write them down. I do the same. My first drafts are always done walking up and down the street, as I said before. When I find that I'm apt to forget, I dictate what I have. If I don't do that, I'm hampered

93

by the fact of having to keep it in my memory. Then I go on, shaping and reshaping.

MAC SHANE: I should like to know about the next stage. How do you go over the lines you have dictated?

DI GIOVANNI: Borges doesn't dictate his Spanish to me.

BORGES: One of the reasons I don't, and I can say it safely here, is that I have a very efficient secretary—efficient in the sense that she is altogether stupid. For example, instead of saying "I am," let's suppose I made the mistake of saying "I is." She would write that down. And my friend di Giovanni can testify to the fact that in reading manuscripts of mine he often and quite suddenly comes upon the words "period" or "semicolon." But I feel quite safe with her and can't make a fool of myself. She is a very nice woman and is very fond of me, which makes things easier. On the other hand, when I attempt dictation to my mother it is quite difficult. She says, "No, this won't do!" or "How on earth could you write that!" That sharp old lady is only ninety-five.

DI GIOVANNI: And there is another reason: I can't take dictation and also do the other work I have to do, so there has to be this division of labor.

BORGES: Why can't you take dictation?

DI GIOVANNI: Because while you are dictating in the morning, I'm at home preparing the work we will do that afternoon.

BORGES: Of course—my mistake. He prepares in the morning and we translate together in the afternoon. Well, he's doing all the work, really.

DI GIOVANNI: But occasionally, on trips, when this wonderful woman isn't with us, I do take dictation. I stand midway between the woman and his mother: I write in semicolons as semicolons, and I don't criticize directly.

BORGES: My mother is very critical of me.

DI GIOVANNI: I do all my criticizing when we make the translation. Borges, I have an idea. Why don't we try out that new poem called "The Watcher"?

BORGES: Yes. In Spanish it is called "El centinela."

The Watcher

The light comes in and I awake. There he is.
He starts by telling me his name, which is (of course) my own.
I return to the slavery that's lasted more than seven times
    ten years.
He thrusts his memory on me.
He thrusts on me the petty drudgery of each day, the fact
    of dwelling in a body.
I am his old nurse; he makes me wash his feet.
He lies in wait for me in mirrors, in mahogany, in
    shopwindows.

Some woman or other has rejected him and I must share
  his hurt.
He now dictates this poem to me, and I do not like it.
He forces me into the hazy apprenticeship of stubborn
  Anglo-Saxon.
He has converted me to the idolatrous worship of dead soldiers,
to whom perhaps I would have nothing to say.
At the last flight of the stairs, I feel him by my side.
He is in my steps, in my voice.
I hate everything about him.
I note with satisfaction that he can barely see.
I'm inside a circular cell and the endless wall is closing in.
Neither of us deceives the other, but both of us are lying.
We know each other too well, inseparable brother.
You drink the water from my cup and eat my bread.
The door of suicide is open, but theologians hold
that I'll be there in the far shadow of the other kingdom,
  waiting for myself.

BORGES: Well, that's that.

DI GIOVANNI: Do you want to speak about the other autobiographical piece?

BORGES: I wrote another piece called "Borges and Myself," and
these two poems are apparently the same. However, there are
some differences. In "Borges and Myself" I am concerned with

the division between the private man and the public man. In "The Watcher" I am interested in the feeling I get every morning when I awake and find that I am Borges. The first thing I do is think of my many worries. Before awakening, I was nobody, or perhaps everybody and everything—one knows so little about sleep—but waking up, I feel cramped, and I have to go back to the drudgery of being Borges. So this is a contrast of a different kind. It is something deep down within myself—the fact that I feel constrained to be a particular individual, living in a particular city, in a particular time, and so on. This might be thought of as a variation on the Jekyll and Hyde motif. Stevenson thought of the division in ethical terms, but here the division is hardly ethical. It is between the high and fine idea of being all things or nothing in particular, and the fact of being changed into a single man. It is the difference between pantheism—for all we know, we are God when we are asleep—and being merely Mr. Borges in New York. Anyway, I should like to make a final observation. Throughout the poem a kind of shift is always taking place between the fact that I am two and the fact that I am one. For example, sometimes I speak of "him," and then at other moments in the poem I am quite alone, surrounded and ringed in by an endless circular world. And then, in the end, I meet myself. There is always this idea of the split personality. Sometimes I fall back on the metaphor of the other, of The Watcher. At other times, he is waiting for me at the top of the staircase, and then in the next line he is inside me, he is my voice, or he is in my face. This kind of game is kept up until the end. Then I say that the door of suicide is open—Stevenson wrote about the open door of suicide in one of his novels, and it was also used by Asturias—but that committing suicide is useless. If I'm immortal, suicide is no good.

DI GIOVANNI: Do you want to make any comment about the switch you made in the last line from the original version? In substance, it went—do you remember?—"You'll be there waiting for me."

BORGES: At first, I wrote, "You'll be there awaiting me." Then I thought that it would be far more effective to say, "I find myself there. . . ." It enforces the idea, as the Scots had it, of the fetch— of a man seeing himself. I think that in Jewish superstition the idea was that if a man met himself—his *Doppelgänger*, as the Germans call it—he would see God. In the similar Scottish superstition, the idea is that if you meet yourself you meet your real self, and this other self is coming to fetch you. That is why the Scottish for *"Doppelgänger"* is "fetch." I think you find something like that in Egyptian religion, where the double is called the "ka," but I am rather shaky about Egyptian mythology.

DI GIOVANNI: I would like to say one more thing about that last line. The poem was printed in its first version. The new idea occurred to Borges while we were at work on the translation, so we changed the line for the English version. Before the poem comes out . . .

BORGES: Or gets out . . .

DI GIOVANNI: . . . in book form in Spanish, it will get another reading, and then Borges can decide which version he likes better.

BORGES: I've decided already: "I'll be waiting for myself."

*Part Three
Translation*

Translation

The translation seminar at Columbia University meets weekly and is devoted to actual work in translation rather than the study of translation. Students working in various languages bring in their work for discussion. Professional translators are invited to preside over individual seminars according to the different languages involved. What unites the work of the group is that everyone is attempting to translate well into English. Most of the students are young poets and prose writers enrolled in the Writing Division of the School of the Arts. All of the translations attempted are literary.

When Borges and Norman Thomas di Giovanni visited the seminar, the discussion began with an explanation of the purpose of the course. Then Borges made a general statement.

BORGES: There is a strange paradox which I thought of this morning, although perhaps I have been thinking about it for years and
years. I think there are two legitimate ways of translating. One
way is to attempt a literal translation, the other is to try a re-creation. The paradox is—and, of course, "paradox" means something
true that at first appearance seems false—that if you are out for
strangeness, if you want, let's say, to astonish the reader, you can do
that by being literal. I will take an obvious example. I know no
Arabic whatever, but I know there's a book known as "The Thousand and One Nights." Now when Jean Antoine Galland did that
into French, he translated it as *Les Mille et une Nuits*. But when
Captain Burton attempted his famous translation, he translated
the title literally. Following the original Arabic word order, he
called his book *The Book of the Thousand Nights and a Night*.
Now there he created something not to be found in the original,
since to anyone who knows Arabic the phrase isn't at all strange;
it's the normal way of saying it. But in English it sounds very
strange, and there is a certain beauty attained, in this case, through
literal translation.

Now let us take the opposite example—where something is
not translated literally and where the translator has wanted to
re-create the original. I suppose you all know the Latin sentence
about science, *"Ars longa, vita brevis."* When Chaucer chose to
put that into English, he did not write, "Art long, life short,"
which would have been rather cut and dried, but he translated it
in this fashion: "The life so short, the craft so long to learn," or

"The lyf so short, the craft so long to lerne." By working in the words "to learn" he gave the line a kind of wistful music not to be found in the original.

These, I think, are quite good examples of legitimate ways of translating. To take another example, in English you say "Good morning," while in Spanish we say, in the plural, *"Buenos dias"*—"Good days." To translate the Spanish literally might produce a certain outlandish strangeness or beauty. But, of course, it all depends on what you are trying to do. If I may speak of my own work, when I am being more or less straightforward in my expression, then I think the translator has the right to rephrase what I've done.

QUESTION: I'd like to know if, when the two of you are working together translating a story into English, you find yourselves being led into something new, so that you're tempted to rewrite it?

DI GIOVANNI: We may improve upon the original from time to time by hitting on a particularly apt word or phrase; or it's possible to improve because the nature of English is such that we can often be more physical or concrete or specific in the translation. But these are not matters of rewriting, which we do not do. Let me give some specific examples of, let's call them, departures from the text. In "Pedro Salvadores," a story set a hundred or more years back and based on historical facts, Borges speaks of his three characters as "A man, a woman, and the overpowering shadow of a dictator. . . ." The dictator is not named because every Argentine reader knows who he is, but for the English-speaking reader that had to be spelled out. At the appropriate place, we inserted into the translation a sentence stating, "The dictator, of course, was Rosas." Near the end of "The Duel" there is a line in the English version that does not occur in the Spanish. Borges had written of the influence on each other of two women painters, then went on to say that this was only natural, since they were fond of each other. In the translation, we were specific about that influence, adding this sentence: "Clara's sunset glows found their way into Marta Pizarro's patios, and Marta's fondness for straight lines simplified the ornateness of Clara's final stage." Of course, I can cite cases in *Doctor Brodie's Report* when in making the translation Borges saw new possibilities and leaped to make small changes in the original. Both the third and fourth printings of *El informe de Brodie* contain these new touches. There is something added at the end of "The Gospel According to Mark." But this was Borges' decision upon hearing his Spanish again several months after completing his story. When we translate from manuscript, as most of *Brodie* was done, I sometimes point out lapses or suggest a touch or two, which we immediately incorporate into the Spanish. In "The Meeting," we wrote some dialogue and a few other sentences directly into the English version and, after we finished it, translated these lines into Spanish for the "original" text.

QUESTION: Is it difficult for you to stick to the original when you're working in collaboration? Isn't there a danger of a new influence coming in?

DI GIOVANNI: No, I have never felt that.

BORGES: We don't think of ourselves as two men when we are working. We are two minds attempting the same goal.

DI GIOVANNI: Also, Borges writes so well and knows so well what he's doing to begin with that there isn't any temptation to write a different story. It's a pleasure to stick to his original.

QUESTION: I wonder why Borges feels the need for a translator when he seems to know English so well.

BORGES: No, no, I respect the English language too much. I wouldn't dare do that by myself.

DI GIOVANNI: It's not easy for me to comment on that in his presence, but since this is a workshop I can say it.

BORGES: You're being very timid.

DI GIOVANNI: Borges' spoken English is unbelievably good, but when he writes English he becomes very stiff and formal. But then, isn't that a tendency we all have?

BORGES: We all want to be Dr. Johnson, I dare say.

DI GIOVANNI: For another thing, Borges learned the language from an English grandmother who left England in the late 1860's. He learned it as a child in the early part of this century—that was some thirty-odd years later.

BORGES: Naturally, I am apt to be old-fashioned; I'm quite Victorian.

DI GIOVANNI: I kid him about his Edwardian English, but in the last three years I've been trying to make a good American of him.

BORGES: No, no. I prefer "lift" to "elevator," and I'm not tempted to speak of "garbage cans" instead of "dust bins."

DI GIOVANNI: But I've taught him to say "crap"—except he won't say it quite that way. He says, "All that, as you say, 'crap.'"

BORGES: "All that, as I say, 'tommy rot.'" Very old-fashioned, I dare say. "Stuff and nonsense."

DI GIOVANNI: Of course, there are also practical reasons for his not translating his own work. On his own, Borges would be neither inclined nor interested in doing it. Nor would he have the time, not to mention the obstacle that his blindness presents. Let me add that it took me many months, being at Borges' side every day, to determine exactly what I could use and what I had to discard of his English. Sometimes, for example, he wavers about whether we should use a word like "direction," which he can't believe is a common word. I've had to convince him that the gerund construction can be employed to advantage in English. It functions quite differently in Spanish, and Borges abhors its use.

QUESTION: How do you deal with modernisms? Are you concerned with purity of language?

BORGES: If I could write eighteenth-century English, that would be my best performance. But I can't. One can't be Addison or Johnson at will.

DI GIOVANNI: He's living contemporaneously. He's modern in spite of himself.

BORGES: I wonder if it's important to be modern.

DI GIOVANNI: But you are, and there's nothing you can do about it.

BORGES: Yes, I suppose I can't help it.

DI GIOVANNI: Anyhow, Borges' new stories are all set back in the Buenos Aires of fifty or sixty years ago . . .

BORGES: Yes, and that makes it easier for me. I'm always being told that people don't talk this way or that, but if I stick to what was happening in a Buenos Aires slum sixty years ago, no one knows quite how the people spoke or what was said. Only a few old-timers like myself, and they've mostly forgotten all about it.

DI GIOVANNI: The question of modernisms simply does not arise in Borges' work. I mean in general, not just in these new stories. There is a kind of timeless quality about his prose. As a writer he is concerned with purity of language—very much so. We follow that concern in the translations without having to think about it. Something else occasionally crops up that is the opposite of modernisms—archaisms. We are far more likely to encounter those. We deliberately gave an archaic flavor to the little tale called "The Two Kings and Their Two Labyrinths." We wanted to make that sound as Borges later described it, as "a page—overlooked by Lane or Burton—out of the *Arabian Nights.*" I steeped myself in Burton while working on the story. "O king of time and crown of the century!"—I think I lifted that straight out of Burton, which is exactly what Borges did in the first place.

QUESTION: What about dialogue? How do you make what originated in Buenos Aires fifty years ago acceptable to the modern ear?

DI GIOVANNI: I think that's an impossible question because almost all translation questions are impossible unless we have the words in front of us and can be specific. Each case is different. To begin with, the whole thing is done by ear; there are no rules.

BORGES: If we go on making sweeping statements we'll get nowhere.

QUESTION: Let me put it a different way. Sometimes in this seminar we've had nineteenth-century texts brought in which have been translated literally and which therefore sound dated. Does di Giovanni contribute an ear which prevents that from happening?

BORGES: What we're aiming at is something like spoken English. Of course, that's impossible, but what we attempt is an imitation of it. We are certainly trying to avoid written English, which is quite different.

DI GIOVANNI: I think dialogue is the easiest of all to translate because it can't be done literally. You have to sound the original in your head and think, "How would I say this in English?" There's no other way. Translation of dialogue is almost always a paraphrase. Of course, there is notoriously little dialogue in Borges' stories. What you often get instead is a narrator orally telling a story in the first person. "Rosendo's Tale," "The Unworthy Friend," and "Juan Muraña" all take this form. The problem here is to make the whole narrative sound as though it were being talked, yet without making it dialogue—or, I should say, monologue. You have to suggest spoken speech while narrating. It's a trick. But mainly it is a writing problem and not really a translating problem at all.

QUESTION: I just want to say something about the question of writing in modern-sounding English. I've been translating Grimm's *Fairy Tales* and my notion was to write an absolutely modern English but to avoid slang as much as possible, since that would destroy the sense of its being an old fairy tale.

DI GIOVANNI: You've got a difficult problem there, because you're taking on something that practically everyone knows. I recently read a modern translation of Grimm, but I found it horrible because it wasn't giving me what I wanted, which was to have the sensation of reading it as a child and recapturing that experience. I missed all the archaic flavor.

QUESTION: But if I use a dated language, if I have the characters "gaze" instead of "look," I've lost everything.

DI GIOVANNI: Your assignment is difficult, compared to mine, because Borges is here and he's contemporary. I can always ask him, "Did you mean 'gaze' or 'look'?" But I don't think deliberately dated language should be used unless you are after special effects such as the one I mentioned in connection with the *Arabian Nights*.

QUESTION: I'd like to ask you to say more about Addison, Swift, and Steele. When you listen to the English of today, do you think there's been a loss compared to those eighteenth-century masters?

BORGES: One thinks of the eighteenth century as being far more civilized. People then were capable of irony, of a certain lightness of touch that we seem to have lost.

DI GIOVANNI: But eighteenth-century prose doesn't exist in a vacuum. It's a reflection of that age just as our prose is of our age. I don't think there's any point in talking about gains or losses.

BORGES: I remember George Moore said that had he to translate Zola's *L'Assommoir* he would avoid all slang, because slang is always contemporary or of a particular place. He said that he would attempt it in eighteenth-century English. I don't know if he was being sincere or merely clever, or trying to be clever. For myself, I would attempt a kind of pure colorless eighteenth-century English.

DI GIOVANNI: I've heard you say that so many times, Borges. Do you really subscribe to it? You always use that example. I'm dead against it, myself.

BORGES: I think slang smacks of a particular place. If you're working on something written in Buenos Aires slang and try to translate it into, let us say, the slang used by hoodlums in the United States, you've got something quite different.

DI GIOVANNI: We tried that once in the story "Streetcorner Man" and it didn't come off very well. Several reviewers thought it sounded like a combination of Damon Runyon and cowboy slang. I'm planning to tone the slang down and retranslate the story for its next appearance in *A Universal History of Infamy*. I am going to do what Borges suggests, make it more colorless, though I am against that as a principle. I think a more skillful translator could transpose the story into an equivalent American slang.

BORGES: That story has another problem for the translator because when I published it I didn't mean it to be realistic. I meant it to be stagy. I wanted the characters to speak as though they were play actors. But somehow it's been taken as a realistic story, and since then I've been attempting to convince people that that wasn't my real aim at all.

DI GIOVANNI: When we translated that story . . .

BORGES: One has to suppress so many things, blushing for shame.

DI GIOVANNI: . . . we were trying to cover up a lot of its weaknesses.

BORGES: We were at the same time feeling ashamed. I was ashamed of myself.

QUESTION: Would you go about confessing these weaknesses if the author weren't sitting beside you?

BORGES: But you should—why not?

DI GIOVANNI: That's an interesting ethical problem. I don't know. I've just finished translating a story by Roberto Arlt, parts of which were so poorly written I would not have considered the story publishable had I translated those parts literally. I went to Arlt's daughter for help, and even she could make little of the passages in question. She told me her father wrote well when he was unselfconscious but that when he was being "the author" he tended to write sloppily.

BORGES: Besides, you might think there is no author, after all. There is only the muse or the Holy Ghost.

DI GIOVANNI: I don't think you should approach texts or authors as sacred objects or be overly conscious that you are translating. I think the work should be looked on as writing in English. It's a pity every translator can't have the experience of working side by side with his author. It has helped me enormously about being free with the original; Borges exhorts me to "Fling it aside and be free!" It also takes the dullness out of translating, to say nothing of providing the luxury of knowing whether you are right or wrong in your interpretation of knotty passages. Anyway, I'm against literal jobs. Some of the greatest translations only touch on the original.

BORGES: FitzGerald, for example.

DI GIOVANNI: Of course, the freer you are the better you have to be.

BORGES: I have no Hebrew, but I always think of the King James version as a very fine translation of the Bible. Maybe it's better than a literal translation could be.

DI GIOVANNI: At this point we're going to play a portion of a tape recording of one of our work sessions. What you will hear is the verbatim exchange between us across the table as we began the story "The Life of Tadeo Isidoro Cruz (1829–1874)." But before playing the tape, I should explain our method.

I first work alone, preparing a handwritten rough draft of the story. Then I bring this to Borges. We work every afternoon, usually at the Argentine National Library. As you will see, I read him a sentence of the Spanish text and afterward a sentence of my draft. Sometimes we feel these sentences are good enough as they stand, and sometimes we revise them extensively. Borges may correct me, I may ask him to clarify, one or the other of us may suggest alternatives or variations. We constantly rephrase, trying to keep our sentences free of cumbersome or indirect constructions. Our concern during this stage is to get all the Spanish into some kind of English, and, in order to do this, I like to be sure I have a complete understanding not only of the text but also of Borges' intentions. As this stage comes to a close, we are not troubled that we may still be fairly literal and makeshift. Often we remain purposely undecided about which word or which of our alternative phrases to use.

After the point recorded on the tape, I take my annotated draft home, type it out, and begin shaping and polishing the sentences. Any reference I make back to the Spanish at this juncture is usually for checking rhythms and emphases. Now my preoccupations are with matters of tone and style. This stage is the most difficult and time-consuming.

The final stage consists of taking my more-or-less finished draft to Borges and reading it to him—this time without reference to the original Spanish.

BORGES: At this stage we try to forget all about the Spanish.

DI GIOVANNI: Our sole aim now is to see that the piece reads as though it were written in English.

BORGES: Of course, there are other possible methods.

DI GIOVANNI: But this is the one that works best for us. Before I begin, you may look at the Spanish text and at the finished English translation, which is the fourth stage of the work. What the tape records is our collaboration in the second stage. Remember that during our discussion I'm hastily writing notes and scrawling changes in the lines on the page before me. When we fall silent, we are not daydreaming but searching for words.

THE SPANISH TEXT	THE FINISHED TRANSLATION
I'm looking for the face I had *Before the world was made.* YEATS, THE WINDING STAIR	*I'm looking for the face I had* *Before the world was made.* YEATS, A WOMAN YOUNG AND OLD
El seis de febrero de 1829, los montoneros que, hostigados ya por Lavalle, marchaban desde el	On the sixth of February, 1829, a troop of gaucho militia, harried all day by Lavalle on their march

Sur para incorporarse a las divisiones de López, hicieron alto en una estancia cuyo nombre ignoraban, a tres o cuatro leguas del Pergamino; hacia el alba, uno de los hombres tuvo una pesadilla tenaz: en la penumbra del galpón, el confuso grito despertó a la mujer que dormía con él.

north to join the army under the command of López, made a halt some nine or ten miles from Pergamino at a ranch whose name they did not know. Along about dawn, one of the men had a haunting nightmare and, in the dim shadows of a shed where he lay sleeping, his confused outcry woke the woman who shared his bed.

DI GIOVANNI: Notice now on the tape how slowly the opening of this particular story went. I think it took us two work sessions on successive days to complete the first paragraph.

BORGES: Let's go back to the past.

DI GIOVANNI: The story is "Biografía de Tadeo Isidoro Cruz (1829–1874)."

BORGES: Those, of course, are fancy dates in order to make the reader unaware of the fact that he's reading a fancy story from *Martín Fierro*.

DI GIOVANNI: Now, the title. How about "The Life of Tadeo Isidoro Cruz," rather than "Biography"?

BORGES: Yes. I used "biography" to make the whole thing more unlike the poem. But as in this case the reader may be quite unaware that any such poem exists, then I think perhaps "The Life" would be better. Perhaps the word *"biografía"* isn't too good a word, either. It's rather priggish.

DI GIOVANNI: Well, "life" has a Saxon ring to it. Now, I checked the epigraph from Yeats: "I'm looking for the face I had/ Before the world was made." You cite the whole book, *The Winding Stair,* and I'd rather cite the single poem to make it easier for anyone who wants to look it up. Actually, it's a poem in many parts, called "A Woman Young and Old."

DI GIOVANNI: The reason for going into all this is that the epigraphs to Borges' stories aren't always printed correctly. I found, for example, that in the epigraph to "The Circular Ruins" the wrong chapter was cited from *Through the Looking-Glass.* In the Spanish-language editions of Borges' work nothing can be taken for granted.

BORGES: But I think that those two lines should be left— because they don't give the story away.

DI GIOVANNI: No, I'm going to use them. The only thing I want to . . .

BORGES: And besides, as the verses are fine—you know, the platonic idea and so on.

DI GIOVANNI: The only thing I want to do is, instead of giving the title of the book it comes from, I want to give the title of the actual poem.

BORGES: Maybe I gave the title of the book because it was a fine title.

DI GIOVANNI: Well, "A Woman Young and Old" isn't bad, either.

BORGES: Besides, as it made me think of the library, with the winding staircases at hand. . . .

DI GIOVANNI: This is a lapse on Borges' part. The story was written eleven years before he came to the National Library.

DI GIOVANNI: *Sí, sí.* Well, shall we begin? *"El seis de febrero de 1829, los montoneros que, hostigados ya por Lavalle, marchaban desde el Sur para incorporarse a las divisiones de López, hicieron alto en una estancia cuyo nombre ignoraban, a tres o cuatro leguas del Pergamino. . . ."* We can start with that. By the way, this precedes the events of the "Poema conjectural" by some six or seven months, doesn't it?

BORGES: Yes, but this happens in the province of Buenos Aires and the other happened in San Juan.

DI GIOVANNI: Well, are they related? Is there a general war going on?

BORGES: Yes, there is.

DI GIOVANNI: What is the relation between those events that happened to Laprida and these events several months earlier, in February?

BORGES: Well, I think that these men were defeated by my great-grandfather—by Suárez—while the others were defeated by Aldao, who was on the Federal side. You might almost say on Rosas' side.

DI GIOVANNI: Which side is Lavalle on here?

BORGES: No, Lavalle is definitely Unitarian. And his second in command was Suárez.

DI GIOVANNI: And López?

BORGES: No, López was an ally of Rosas, since he was one of the great caudillos of Santa Fe.

DI GIOVANNI: All right, that gives me a little background. Let's see what we can make out of this now.

BORGES: So these men are *montoneros,* they're not real soldiers.

DI GIOVANNI: Well, do you suppose we can use the same term we used in the "Conjectural Poem"—"gaucho militia"?

BORGES: That's it, yes.

DI GIOVANNI: All right. *"El seis de febrero de 1829"*—"On the sixth of February, 1829 . . ."

BORGES: Yes, because I looked out the dates; I looked out the dates for the battle in some handbook or other of Argentine history. *El combate de las Palmitas.*

DI GIOVANNI: Well, "On the sixth of February, 18 . . ."

BORGES: Not too imposing words, no?

DI GIOVANNI: Which?

BORGES: *Las Palmitas.*

DI GIOVANNI: No. "On the sixth of February, 1829 . . ."

BORGES: Of course, they were the name of the *estancia.*

DI GIOVANNI: I see.

BORGES: All those names were the names of the *estancias* where the engagements took place.

DI GIOVANNI: *"Los montoneros que, hostigados ya por Lavalle . . ."*

BORGES: That's right.

DI GIOVANNI: Now, the gaucho militia's on one side, Lavalle's on the other; the gaucho militia are *federales,* and Lavalle is Unitarian.

BORGES: Yes.

DI GIOVANNI: "The gaucho militia who, *hostigados ya por Lavalle . . ."*

BORGES: Well, *"hostigado"* is to be "harrowed" or "harassed" or . . .

DI GIOVANNI: "Pursued" or . . . ?

BORGES: Yes. [*Very long pause.*] Troops that are—that have to be moving . . .

DI GIOVANNI: Yes, continuously, because they are being beset.

BORGES: Yes.

DI GIOVANNI: "Pressed"?

BORGES: Yes.

DI GIOVANNI: All right, I'll find the word for that.

BORGES: *"Hostigar"* comes from *"hostis"* and "hostile" and that kind of thing. The same word as "guest," by the way. Because a "guest" and also *"hostis"*—enemy—both words stood for a stranger; you thought of a stranger as being an enemy.

DI GIOVANNI: And we were translating this story against a deadline!

DI GIOVANNI: Bueno, *"marchaban desde el Sur para incorporarse a las divisiones de López"*— "were marching south . . ."

BORGES: No, on the contrary—*"desde el Sur"*—"were marching north."

DI GIOVANNI: "Were marching from the south."

BORGES: Well, or "north." But they came from the—they may have come from near Dolores and [*indecipherable*] from the southern parts of the province.

DI GIOVANNI: All right, "were marching from the south"— "*para incorporarse a las divisiones de López*"— "to join López' divisions," no?

BORGES: Yes.

DI GIOVANNI: "*Incorporarse*"?

BORGES: "*Incorporarse*," yes. Or even "López' army" might be better, no?

DI GIOVANNI: All right, "López' army."

BORGES: Also an army of *montoneros*.

DI GIOVANNI: But that's what they were aiming to do—to join up, no?

BORGES: Yes, that's it, yes.

DI GIOVANNI: "*Hicieron alto en una estancia cuyo nombre ignoraban a tres o cuatro leguas del Pergamino.*"— "Made a halt at a ranch whose name they did not know . . ."

BORGES: Yes.

DI GIOVANNI: ". . . some ten or twelve miles from Pergamino."

BORGES: That's right, yes.

DI GIOVANNI: Perhaps "outside of Pergamino," no?

BORGES: Yes.

DI GIOVANNI: But I see now that I was mistaken and that Borges was inattentive here. It should have been *the* Pergamino, the stream, and not Pergamino, the town, which probably didn't exist in 1829.

DI GIOVANNI: *"Hacia el alba, uno de los hombres tuvo una pesadilla tenaz: en la penumbra del galpón, el confuso grito despertó a la mujer que dormía con él."*

BORGES: So then we are just told that he had a woman with him, no?

DI GIOVANNI: *Sí. Bueno. "Hacia el alba"*— "Along about dawn . . ."

BORGES: Yes, that's right.

DI GIOVANNI: *". . . uno de los hombres tuvo una pesadilla tenaz"*—"one of the men had a . . ."

BORGES: Well, you wouldn't say "tenacious."

DI GIOVANNI: "Bad nightmare," no?

BORGES: Or a "bad dream." A "bad nightmare," yes.

DI GIOVANNI: "A bad nightmare:"— *"en la penumbra del galpón el confuso grito despertó a la mujer que dormía con él."* The *"galpón"* is the shed where he's sleeping, no?

BORGES: Yes.

DI GIOVANNI: Right. "In the deep shadows of the shed," or "in the darkness"?

BORGES: "In the darkness," yes.

DI GIOVANNI: Yes, "in the darkness."

BORGES: But *"penumbra,"* of course, would be a kind of—well, it would be towards the dawn.

DI GIOVANNI: What's that? Dawn?

BORGES: Well, near the daybreak. Because it's *"penumbra"*— I mean, it's . . .

DI GIOVANNI: Well, how about "dim shadows," which gives an idea that it's coming light, no? "In the dim shadows of the shed, his confused"— *"confuso grito"*— "his confused out-cry"?

BORGES: "Outcry," yes.

DI GIOVANNI: Yes. "Woke the woman who shared his bed."

BORGES: Yes. Of course, there are no beds; they're sleeping . . .

DI GIOVANNI: Well, that's figurative. They're sleeping on the ground, no?

BORGES: Yes, of course, on the ground; they didn't have any beds.

DI GIOVANNI: We were interrupted by a visitor here, and that was all the work we did that first afternoon. All told, we'd had an eleven- or twelve-minute session. Now we'll have the next day.

DI GIOVANNI: We're back to our friend Isidoro Tadeo. Now, I went to work on those first sentences that we started with yesterday, so I'll start by reading you those, and then we'll swing right in . . .

BORGES: I know, because those were rather involved.

DI GIOVANNI: Well, look, here's what I've got now for the opening couple of lines. I'll read them very slowly. "On the sixth of February, 1829, the troop of gaucho militia, harried all day by Lavalle on their march north to join the army under the command of López, made a halt some nine or ten miles from Pergamino, at a ranch whose name was unknown to them."

BORGES: Yes, that was the Acevedo ranch. Go on.

DI GIOVANNI: "Along about dawn, one of the men had a haunting nightmare"— for *"tenaz."*

BORGES: That's good. "Haunting" is good, yes.

DI GIOVANNI: "There in the dim shadows of a shed where he lay asleep, his confused outcry woke the woman who shared his bed." Now I checked up on this "bed." "Bed" doesn't necessarily have to mean literally the furniture.

BORGES: No, because if not it would make it too gorgeous.

DI GIOVANNI: Yes, but the thing is, you bed down with a woman, it means—it doesn't mean you've bought yourself a fancy . . .

BORGES: It doesn't mean—it doesn't stand for bedposts and curtains.

DI GIOVANNI: Right. So I think that sets the opening.

DI GIOVANNI: I think that will do. Thankfully, the work went faster after that, but here at the beginning it was really tough. Our aim was to make the reader see the sides clearly, even if he didn't understand the issues. I'm glad to say that since that story was translated, over a year ago, we've done many others with historical backgrounds, so that I find them easier now.

MAC SHANE: Would you tell us something about the autobiographical piece and how this collaboration differed from translation? Did you use the same method of sitting down together?

BORGES: I think we were more at ease.

DI GIOVANNI: To begin with, we weren't burdened by an original text. But we really worked much the same way. Our first task was to make a simple outline of Borges' life— 1. when and where born; 2. father; 3. mother; 4. ancestors; and so on. I even dictated the first sentence to get Borges started. Then he just spoke it out to me, dictating. When he hesitated, I'd say, "Don't jump to your ancestors yet, we're talking about your father." That way. Or I'd want to know exactly what brought his English grandmother to South America. Once the work got rolling, it was easy for me to anticipate him, and so I could make suggestions and at times take down my own dictation, which he would approve. The great task in the beginning was to keep Borges to the outline, because he sometimes wanders and digresses a great deal.

BORGES: You people here know all about that already.

DI GIOVANNI: No, the idea was to make him talk, while I, with paper and pencil in hand, shaped and guided. I tried to get the memories to flow.

BORGES: Now I am remembering all the time.

DI GIOVANNI: Then at night I'd go home and do the research, making sure the dates and facts were correct.

BORGES: Of course, the dates were always wrong.

DI GIOVANNI: No, you never had any dates. When I asked him what year something had taken place, he'd say, "I don't know; ask my mother, she's only ninety-five." In addition to the researching, I'd also type up the day's dictation and begin shaping it, just as in the translations. After we had a rough draft of a chapter, we'd go back and polish and give it final form. In this way, the work took us . . .

BORGES: Quite some time.

DI GIOVANNI: I think it took us three months, working even Saturdays and Sundays. It may be worth telling what started us on the autobiography. We were preparing *The Aleph and Other Stories,* an anthology of short stories, but were having trouble getting rights to make new translations of certain essential material. So with the manuscript due but looking rather thin to me, I thought we would refurbish and add to the book a talk Borges had given on himself at the University of Oklahoma several months before. But when I looked at the transcript, my heart sank. What had made a fine talk was worthless on the page. The material jumped around too much and was without a single date to guide the reader. When I told Borges this, he simply shrugged it off and said to throw the text away and we'd start from scratch. We salvaged exactly half of one sentence from the Oklahoma talk, and we went on to write a sixty-odd page piece. I was amazed by Borges' alacrity—toss it away and let's start over—when I felt utterly defeated. But we fell behind publishing schedule; I had corrected proofs for the stories and we hadn't finished the autobiography yet. And then we had to write the little commentaries that filled out the volume. Those alone took us another month. Of course, along the way there were interruptions.

BORGES: Sometimes these interruptions were simply my laziness.

DI GIOVANNI: Not at all.

BORGES: I'm constitutionally lazy.

DI GIOVANNI: I meant other interruptions. We finished the work while Borges was lecturing in the south of the province of Buenos Aires. I remember reading him copy at the top of my voice over the motors of our twin-engine plane. Then we finished in a hotel, Borges sprawled out on the bed, me bent over the night table, which was my desk. It was an enormous relief to come to the end with all those pressures bearing down. We were forced to correct the New Yorker's proof of the piece by telephone.

Oh, yes, I also remember that the only argument we've ever had occurred while writing the autobiography. I wanted Borges to discuss the three books of essays he had written in the twenties and has never allowed to be reprinted. He said no, that he wanted to forget all about them. I argued that we couldn't just jump over several years of his life that way. "Why not," he said, "whose life is this?" I told him I didn't mind if he condemned the books, but I thought he had to speak of them; then I read what he had dictated to me about them several days earlier. He liked what I read back and said he'd mention the books if he could leave their titles out. That seemed to underline his condemnation, which would be a fine touch, so I agreed wholeheartedly. We came close to another argument when I wanted him to tell what his daily life was like while he worked at the municipal library in the early forties. He could not see what bearing that had on anything nor of what interest it would be to anyone. I told him firmly that it interested me and would interest his American readers—after all, he was doing his finest work at that time. He relented without another word, and I was glad because I think those are the piece's best and certainly most moving pages.

MAC SHANE: When you are translating, do you refer to other translations?

DI GIOVANNI: No, because I don't want anybody else's words or solutions in my head. I'm lucky because I'd never read Borges before I started translating him. And I don't read any studies of his work. If you once read what the professors say about his work, you won't translate another line. They make such a fuss about hidden meanings.

BORGES: I'm a professor myself, and I know all about that.

QUESTION: I wonder if I could ask a devil's advocate question. I know there are two or more versions of some of Borges' work, and I wonder what both of you think of _____ _____'s translations.

BORGES: We must tell the gentleman that _____'s versions are far better than our own, no?

DI GIOVANNI: Far better than our own.

BORGES: It's only too obvious.

131

DI GIOVANNI: I wanted to crib from his versions, but Borges said, "No, it's his work; it would be unethical." [Many of Borges' translators, incidentally, have tended to be literal, taking the first English word suggested by the Spanish.] Another translation of the story we just listened in on, for example, calls it "The Biography of Tadeo Isidoro Cruz."

BORGES: Yes, and when I say "dark" . [when he says "dark"

DI GIOVANNI: They always say "obscure."

BORGES: Instead of a "dark room" for *"una habitación oscura,"* you get "an obscure habitation."

DI GIOVANNI: But the trick is to get that "tenacious nightmare" of the original to "bad nightmare" or "bad dream" of the rough draft to the final "haunting nightmare." And, of course, that boils down to a writing problem.]

On the next part of the tape there's a long discussion of the word *"leguas,"* which we translated as "miles."

MAC SHANE: You don't use "leagues"?

BORGES: In the Argentine, yes.

DI GIOVANNI: But in our translations we try to use ordinary English terms. The word *"legua,"* I found, means anything from 2.4 to 4.6 miles. That's not very helpful. But Borges clearly remembered that a *"legua"* is forty *"cuadras,"* or blocks, and that each city block was laid out a hundred meters long. So the

Argentine league came out to four thousand meters. This is important because later on in the story we are told that the cavalry has been on a chase of over twenty miles. If we'd given it as fifty miles they'd have required very strong horses. We try to take pains over details like this.

BORGES: Of course, my grandfather was a great rider.

DI GIOVANNI: But if I remember correctly, you told me that if we were going to err, we should do so on the short side so as not to make the facts unlikely.

QUESTION: In the autobiographical essay, you say that when you were nine or so you translated Oscar Wilde's "The Happy Prince." Was it a good translation, do you think?

BORGES: I wonder. I'll have to look into it. It was accepted and published, you know.

DI GIOVANNI: I spent two days trying to find it, going through four or five years of newspapers. I suspect it's not within those dates we gave in the essay. I worked his age out with his mother, and he was probably a year or two older—ten or so. But to publish a translation in a metropolitan newspaper even at the age of ten is quite an achievement.

BORGES: Oscar Wilde is the easiest writer to translate. His English was very simple. At that time, I knew many sentences of *The Picture of Dorian Gray* by heart.

DI GIOVANNI: We're now going to have a look at a couple of brief examples of translation. The first is merely a diversion; it's the label from a ketchup bottle that I found in Buenos Aires. It is obviously a transliteration made with the dictionary, and I take this to be the lowest form of translation.

BORGES: The lowest and funniest.

DI GIOVANNI: The second example consists of two sentences—or two forms of the same sentence—and this is really my whole textbook on translation. Here is the first form; it is from a story by Borges:

The torrential rains, Captain Liddell Hart comments, caused this delay, an insignificant one, to be sure.

The other form reads:

Captain Liddell Hart comments that this delay, an insignificant one to be sure, was caused by torrential rains.

I would like us to judge this as translation without referring to the original. It's plain that the second form is better. As a matter of fact, it is simply a rewriting of the first. It should be obvious that the elements of the first sentence are put together all wrong. They are not forceful. A good sentence in English has a structure that begins with the second most important element, moves to the least important element, and ends with the strongest element. The pattern is 2–3–1. The second sentence follows this rule. But notice how limp the first example is. So my whole thesis on translation is that you must write good sentences—effective English. That's all there is to it.

QUESTION: Would the word order in the original probably be different?

DI GIOVANNI: From the first example, no. The translator was scrupulously literal. But when I translate I am concerned with the English sentence structure, not the Spanish. I don't know much about sentence structure in Spanish, but I know that a construction that may be the same in both languages does not necessarily produce the same effect in each: the gerund, for example. In English, it adds immediacy and speeds a sentence up; in Spanish, it is cumbersome and impeding. To follow Borges' sentence structure in translation can be treacherous. He has changed the Spanish language; his sentence structure is largely modeled on English, and you may be able to reel off four consecutive sentences in English just following his Spanish. But the fifth has a Spanish structure; follow it and the English is killed.

QUESTION: I don't know about the structure of Spanish sentences either, but I think a contortion in English would affect me much more than a straightforward sentence. Don't you want to maintain something of that?

BORGES: When I write, I play by ear. I attempt a sentence, and then I read it over again. If it sounds unnatural, I change it. There are no set rules of any kind.

DI GIOVANNI: It all depends on what effect you think the sentence was meant to have in the original. In the example, no contortion was intended. The worst problem in translation is to translate something that is badly written in the original. If you translate it as it is, you're criticized for making a bad translation.

BORGES: I remember, when I translated Faulkner's *Wild Palms,* that people told me the sentences were far too involved, and I was blamed for that.

QUESTION: I have a question about *The Aleph and Other Stories.* In the preface, you say, "We do not consider English and Spanish as compounded of sets of easily interchangeable synonyms; they are two quite different ways of looking at the world, each with a nature of its own." Is it possible, then, that there are certain stories or certain pieces of literature that are impossible to translate?

BORGES: In the case of a story, no; in the case of poetry, of course. There is always something left with a story.

QUESTION: There are no stories you consider untranslatable because they reflect a peculiarly Spanish way of looking at the world?

BORGES: No, I don't think so. I don't think I have a Spanish way of looking at the world. I've done most of my reading in English.

DI GIOVANNI: Borges' Spanish is already much more specific than anyone else's. That's one of the reasons it is a delight to translate him into English and why he loses so little in translation. I listen to a sentence of his and I can hear an English sentence beneath it. As I've said, many times his syntax isn't really Spanish. And he has introduced verb forms seldom used before in the language—the present perfect tense. He has revitalized the language.

BORGES: Thank you.

DI GIOVANNI: No, don't thank me. García Márquez is thanking you; Carlos Fuentes is thanking you. People ask me how I reflect in English what Borges has done to Spanish. In English, the adjective precedes the noun—"black dog"—whereas in Spanish it's usually the other way around. But Borges has put the adjective in front of the noun. Obviously, I'm not going to translate that "dog black." In a way, since English made Borges and since he is giving Spanish an English cast, he fulfills himself in English, his work becomes more itself in English.

QUESTION: What happens in translating his poetry?

DI GIOVANNI: That's a very different problem. Next year we're publishing a book of one hundred selected poems. I'm the editor, and, in all, some twelve translators are involved. After making the selection together, Borges and I sat down and wrote a literal draft for every poem. I then began commissioning poets and worked with them whenever necessary, providing notes and explanations and sometimes the literal versions. Richard Wilbur, who does not know Spanish, though he has translated widely from the French, was provided with these aids; so was John Updike. They produced some absolutely beautiful sonnets for us.

BORGES: Who translated "Deathwatch on the Southside"?

DI GIOVANNI: Robert Fitzgerald. He worked from a version he had published in 1942, which was the second time Borges had ever appeared in English. But Borges had subsequently revised the original, so I asked Fitzgerald to revise his translation to conform with Borges' changes. With Borges at hand, we had a chance to clear up many obscure and difficult things in the poem. Fitzgerald got caught up with the work and produced an entirely new version. Almost everything was done by letter, and the correspondence is incredibly voluminous. It's taken us three years to do this book.

So, first of all, there is a difference in method between the prose and the poetry. Another difference is that the prose pieces are all signed as having been done in collaboration. The poems are not signed that way because at some point they are no longer collaborations. There are many elements in the poems—English meter is one—that Borges doesn't understand or care about, and so I am on my own, and Borges has to take my solutions on faith. Obviously, there are many poems where the problems are simple and we are in complete agreement. When we work with other poets, we use the literal versions as a control. When necessary, as I've said, we send these word-by-word renderings together with thorough notes to the prospective translator.

BORGES: And he makes it into poetry.

DI GIOVANNI: Even the poets who know Spanish are sometimes grateful for these transliterations. With them, they don't have to waste time interpreting the poem. The plain meaning is given them, and they can sail right into the poetry. It's a discouraging thing to make a mistake and then base a poetic line on it, only to have someone else come along and say, "I'm sorry, but Borges says you're wrong; it's not 'the south of Argentina,' it's 'the South-side of Buenos Aires.'" Even Bill Merwin, who has translated a lot from Spanish, asked me for these literal versions.

BORGES: Yes, because even though you may know Spanish or Mexican Spanish, you may be quite unaware of something's being different in Argentine or Uruguayan Spanish.

DI GIOVANNI: Yes, in one story the Uruguayan word for the maté kettle—"caldera"—is translated as "soup cauldron," its meaning in Spain. Also, Borges has his own peculiarities. When he says "tarde," he usually means "evening" and seldom "afternoon," and

139

the reason for this is that in Buenos Aires the afternoons are very hot and no one but a mad dog or an Englishman would be out in the streets.

BORGES: I never thought of that, but maybe you're right.

DI GIOVANNI: It was you who told me. Anyhow, since afternoon is a time for sleep, *"tarde"* is the evening, when you wake up. It's nice to know these personal usages of Borges'.

QUESTION: Do you work together while translating a poem?

DI GIOVANNI: I bring Borges a rough draft, and we go over it to make sure I've got the literal sense straight. Sometimes the lines are fine as they are. Once we did a free-verse poem in twenty minutes, but that was because the subject matter was so close to English it just came out, one word after another, very easily. This was "Invocation to Joyce," which in subject is much closer to English than to Spanish. It's interesting what happens when a theme is more suitable to English. Once, in another poem, "Hengest Cyning," an Anglo-Saxon figure, I was able to use alliteration, and it worked beautifully.

BORGES: In Spanish it can hardly be done, or it will be spotted as a trick. But in English it's part of the language. Shakespeare and Swinburne have both used alliteration.

MAC SHANE: What do you do about rhyme? I know that in translating some of Borges' sonnets, Richard Howard used unrhymed syllabic verse instead.

BORGES: The trouble with rhyme in English is that the accent usually falls on the first syllable: *"cour*age," which in French would be "cour*age."* The Latin languages therefore are easier to rhyme.

DI GIOVANNI: The several translators found different solutions for handling rhyme. John Hollander did a heroic job on a long poem of quatrains. Bill Ferguson and Richard Wilbur rhymed their sonnets. But we mostly settled for blank verse, closed occasionally with a rhymed couplet. Rhyme is hardly poetry, and we found it quite expendable.

I'd now like to read the translation of "Invocación a Joyce."

Invocation to Joyce

Scattered over scattered cities,
alone and many
we played at being that Adam
who gave names to all living things.
Down the long slopes of night
that border on the dawn,
we sought (I still remember) words
for the moon, for death, for the morning,
and for man's other habits.
We were imagism, cubism,
the conventicles and sects
respected now by credulous universities.
We invented the omission of punctuation

and capital letters,
stanzas in the shape of a dove
from the librarians of Alexandria.
Ashes, the labor of our hands,
and a burning fire our faith.
You, all the while,
in cities of exile,
in that exile that was
your detested and chosen instrument,
the weapon of your craft,
erected your pathless labyrinths,
infinitesimal and infinite,
wondrously paltry,
more populous than history.
We shall die without sighting
the twofold beast or the rose
that are the center of your maze,
but memory holds its talismans,
its echoes of Virgil,
and so in the streets of night
your splendid hells survive,
so many of your cadences and metaphors,
the treasures of your darkness.
What does our cowardice matter if on this earth
there is one brave man,
what does sadness matter if in time past
somebody thought himself happy,

what does my lost generation matter,
that dim mirror,
if your books justify us?
I am the others. I am all those
who have been rescued by your pains and care.
I am those unknown to you and saved by you.

The one word in the poem I had to search for was "pathless,"
in the line "erected your pathless labyrinths." The Spanish was
"tus arduos laberintos." I'm afraid Borges has worked the word
"arduo" to death.

Now here is the other extreme. It's a poem called "John 1:14."
It took me a year to translate. I don't mean I worked on it every
day, but I would work to exhaustion over a period of two or three
days and then put it away. A year had passed before it was finished.

John 1:14

This page will be no less a riddle
than those of My holy books
or those others repeated
by ignorant mouths
believing them the handiwork of a man,
not the Spirit's dark mirrors.
I who am the Was, the Is, and the Is To Come
again condescend to the written word,
which is time in succession and no more than an emblem.

Who plays with a child plays with something
near and mysterious;
wanting once to play with My children,
I stood among them with awe and tenderness.
I was born of a womb
by an act of magic.
I lived under a spell, imprisoned in a body,
in the humbleness of a soul.
I knew memory,
that coin that's never twice the same.
I knew hope and fear,
those twin faces of the uncertain future.
I knew wakefulness, sleep, dreams,
ignorance, the flesh,
reason's roundabout labyrinths,
the friendship of men,
the blind devotion of dogs.
I was loved, understood, praised, and hung from a cross.
I drank My cup to the dregs.
My eyes saw what they had never seen—
night and its many stars.
I knew things smooth and gritty, uneven and rough,
the taste of honey and apple,
water in the throat of thirst,
the weight of metal in the hand,
the human voice, the sound of footsteps on the grass,
the smell of rain in Galilee,

the cry of birds on high.
I knew bitterness as well.
I have entrusted the writing of these words to a common man;
they will never be what I want to say
but only their shadow.
These signs are dropped from My eternity.
Let someone else write the poem, not he who is now its scribe.
Tomorrow I shall be a great tree in Asia,
or a tiger among tigers
preaching My law to the tiger's woods.
Sometimes homesick, I think back
on the smell of that carpenter's shop.

When this poem was taken by the *New Yorker,* Howard
Moss made a valuable suggestion about one of the lines. The Spanish read, *"Por obra de una magia/ nací curiosamente de un vien-
tre."* In English, I had written, "I was strangely born of a womb/
by an act of magic." Howard pointed out that "strangely" and "by
an act of magic" was a redundancy, and so I gratefully cut the
word. When Borges and I prepare the bilingual edition of *In
Praise of Darkness* for Dutton, I'll take this up with him, and he
may wish to drop the word from the original as well. This, incidentally, is an example of why I can't sign the poems as collaborations. I took that cut upon myself without consulting Borges. Of
course, I always read the final draft to him, and he always gives
his okay, though sometimes with reservations. When that happens,
I ask him to take a word or line of mine on faith.

I'd now like us to have a look at two versions of a poem called "A Page to Commemorate Colonel Suárez, Victor at Junín." Alastair Reid published this version of the poem in *A Personal Anthology:*

A Page to Commemorate Colonel Suárez, Victor at Junín

What do they matter now, the deprivations,
the alienation, the frustrations of growing old,
the dictator's shadow spreading across the land, the house
in the Barrio del Alto, which his brothers sold while
    he fought,
the useless days
(those one hopes to forget, those one knows are forgettable),
when he had, at least, his burning hour, on horseback
on the clear plains of Junín, a setting for the future?

What matters the flow of time, if he knew
that fullness, that ecstasy, that afternoon?

He served three years in the American Wars; and then
luck took him to Uruguay, to the banks of the Río Negro.
In the dying afternoons, he would think
that somehow, for him, a rose had burst into flower,
taken flesh in the battle of Junín, the ever-extending moment
when the lances clashed, the order which shaped the battle,
the initial defeat, and in the uproar
(no less harsh for him than for the army),

his voice crying out at the attacking Peruvians,
the light, the force, the fatefulness of the charge,
the teeming labyrinths of foot soldiers,
the crossing of lances, when no shot resounded,
the Spaniard fighting with a reckless sword,
the victory, the luck, the exhaustion, a dream beginning,
and the men dying among the swamps,
and Bolívar uttering words which were marked for history,
and the sun, in the west by now, and, anew, the taste
of wine and water,
and death, that death without a face,
for the battle had trampled over it, effaced it . . .

His great-grandson is writing these lines,
and a silent voice comes to him out of the past,
out of the blood:

"What does my battle at Junín matter if it is only
a glorious memory, or a date learned by rote
for an examination, or a place in the atlas?
The battle is everlasting, and can do without
the pomp of the obvious armies with their trumpets;
Junín is two civilians cursing a tyrant
on a street corner,
or an unknown man somewhere, dying in prison."

I liked the translation enough to ask Alastair if he would revise it.
When he agreed to, I sent him four or five single-spaced typewrit-

ten pages of suggestions, but I was fearful of his reaction. Instead, he wrote back elated, swearing he'd never translate another line of Borges without my being between him and the text. There I'd been worried about how he'd take our criticism and he was marvelous; a look at his later poem shows how unstinting he was in his efforts.

Now, Alastair knew that Colonel Suárez was an Argentine officer, but in line two of the first version, using the word "alienation," he must have assumed that Suárez was somehow not getting along in his own country. In fact, the man was living in exile in Uruguay.

QUESTION: What was the original word?

BORGES: *"Destierro."*

DI GIOVANNI: The translator didn't realize what was going on because of the poem's hidden roots in Argentine history. In the ninth and tenth lines, for example, it's not a "flow of time," but quite the opposite. Suárez was living apart from his own countrymen, and time wasn't flowing, it was a monotony. Farther along, we suggested Alastair use the phrase "Wars of Independence" instead of "American Wars," because that's what they're called. A few lines later, the first version reads, "luck took him to Uruguay." Well, the Spanish word is *"suerte,"* and of course it means "luck," but it also means "fate," and that's the correct reading here, since it's obviously not a man's "luck" that sends him into exile. All of this misreading so far comes from a lack of historical and biographical information.

BORGES: Which in the original is all taken for granted.

DI GIOVANNI: There's a crucial mistake a few lines farther on, where the first version reads, "his voice crying out at the attacking Peruvians." Although Suárez was an Argentine, he was leading Peruvians. Otherwise it would seem that there were a war between the two countries; but the fact is that they were allies against the Spaniards.

Another mistake occurs a few lines later, where Alastair wrote "labyrinths of foot soldiers"—the original being *"laberintos de ejércitos."* But the battle was fought entirely on horseback. How was the translator to know that? Borges does not say so. We suggested this be changed to "cavalries." Here is Reid's second version of the poem, made for Borges' *Selected Poems 1923–1967:*

A Page to Commemorate Colonel Suárez, Victor at Junín

What do they matter now, the deprivations,
exile, the ignominies of growing old,
the dictator's shadow spreading across the land, the house
in the Barrio del Alto, which his brothers sold while
    he fought,
the pointless days (days one hopes to forget,
days one knows are forgettable),
when he had at least his burning hour on horseback
on the plateau of Junín, a stage for the future,
as if that mountain stage itself were the future?

What is time's monotony to him, who knew
that fulfillment, that ecstasy, that afternoon?

Thirteen years he served in the Wars of Independence. Then
fate took him to Uruguay, to the banks of the Río Negro.
In the dying afternoons he would think
of his moment which had flowered like a rose—
the crimson battle of Junín, the enduring moment
in which the lances crossed, the order of battle,
defeat at first, and in the uproar
(as astonishing to him as to the army)
his voice urging the Peruvians to the attack,
the thrill, the drive, the decisiveness of the charge,
the seething labyrinth of cavalries,
clash of the lances (not a single shot fired),
the Spaniard he ran through with his spear,
the headiness of victory, the exhaustion, the drowsiness
        descending,
and the men dying in the marshes,
and Bolívar uttering words earmarked no doubt for history,
and the sun in the west by now, and water and wine
tasted as for the first time, and that dead man
whose face the battle had trampled on and obliterated. . . .

His great-grandson is writing these lines,
and a silent voice comes to him out of the past,
out of the blood:

"What does my battle at Junín matter if it is only
a glorious memory, or a date learned by rote
for an examination, or a place in the atlas?
The battle is everlasting and can do without
the pomp of actual armies and of trumpets.
Junín is two civilians cursing a tyrant
on a street corner,
or an unknown man somewhere, dying in prison."

Looking at the two, I think the poem is much sharper and stronger
in the later version. And it simply could not have been done without Borges there to guide it.

BORGES: I published that poem in *Sur,* and, naturally, I was thinking of an audience that would know about these things.

DI GIOVANNI: Another of my jobs has been to match poems with
translators. I wouldn't send a poem in free verse to Wilbur, and I
wouldn't send a sonnet to Merwin. In Richard Howard's case, he
was working at the time on his *Untitled Subjects,* which is a series
of long nineteenth-century biographical portraits. It was obvious
that I give him Borges' sonnets on nineteenth-century figures.
Richard did poems on Whitman, Heine, Swedenborg, Poe, and so
forth. He also got me interested in syllabic meter, which I used to
translate "Conjectural Poem," which in Spanish is written in hen-
decasyllables—eleven-syllable lines.

BORGES: Which come out ten syllables in English.

DI GIOVANNI: But I didn't feel the poem could be translated into pentameter without torturing it. I did the first draft as free verse, and saw that the lines very nearly matched the Spanish in length.

BORGES: *"Corrientes, aguas puras, cristalinas. . . ."*

DI GIOVANNI: So in the end I went back and shaped each line into ten syllables. This is not something you can hear when the lines are read, but it nonetheless gives a certain restraint and subtlety to the poem.

Conjectural Poem

> Doctor Francisco Laprida, set upon and
> killed the 22nd of September 1829
> by a band of gaucho militia serving
> under Aldao, reflects before he dies:

Bullets whip the air this last afternoon.
A wind is up, blowing full of cinders
as the day and this chaotic battle
straggle to a close. The gauchos have won:
victory is theirs, the barbarians'.
I, Francisco Narciso Laprida,
who studied both canon law and civil
and whose voice declared the independence
of this entire untamed territory,
in defeat, my face marked by blood and sweat,
holding neither hope nor fear, the way lost,
strike out for the South through the back country.

Like that captain in *Purgatorio*
who fleeing on foot left blood on the plain
and was blinded and then trampled by death
where an obscure river loses its name,
so I too will fall. Today is the end.
The night and to right and left the marshes—
in ambush, clogging my steps. I hear the
hooves of my own hot death riding me down
with horsemen, frothing muzzles, and lances.

I who longed to be someone else, to weigh
judgments, to read books, to hand down the law,
will lie in the open out in these swamps;
but a secret joy somehow swells my breast.
I see at last that I am face to face
with my South American destiny.
I was carried to this ruinous hour
by the intricate labyrinth of steps
woven by my days from a day that goes
back to my birth. At last I've discovered
the mysterious key to all my years,
the fate of Francisco de Laprida,
the missing letter, the perfect pattern
that was known to God from the beginning.
In this night's mirror I can comprehend
my unsuspected true face. The circle's
about to close. I wait to let it come.

My feet tread the shadows of the lances
that spar for the kill. The taunts of my death,
the horses, the horsemen, the horses' manes,
tighten the ring around me. . . . Now the first
blow, the lance's hard steel ripping my chest,
and across my throat the intimate knife.

In another version of this poem, there's an amazing howler.
In Spanish, the word *"casco"* means both "helmet" and "hoof."
The poem, as we've seen, is full of horses. Nevertheless, the translator had the line, "I hear the helmets of my fiery death seeking
me out." This has now become a little joke between Borges and
me, and whenever the word *"casco"* comes up in our work, if it
means "hoof" I say "helmet" and if it means "helmet" I say "hoof."

BORGES: The fellow who translated that had Spanish as his native
language. I remember I told him once before a public reading of
the translation, "Look here, *'cascos'* is 'hoofs.' "

DI GIOVANNI: Borges had told the man this at a noon reading, and
that evening the man read his translation again without changing
the word. He obviously knew better than the author. Anyhow,
this is such a common failing. Often translators don't think, they
just put down words without remembering that horses don't nor-
mally wear helmets. Or else they think too much and fall under
the perverse spell of surrealism.

MAC SHANE: Do you ever put a story away for a month before
finishing it?

DI GIOVANNI: No, I don't think that's quite necessary in translation, though it seems to me a good idea with original writing.

MAC SHANE: But if you get too close to a work, don't you get blind to it?

DI GIOVANNI: But don't forget, we are two people, and what I miss Borges catches, and vice versa. Also, there are other factors involved. I often have to meet deadlines, and so such a luxury isn't always possible. There have, however, been one or two cases when I've sent a story out for three or four months and seen it repeatedly rejected, only to discover—upon rereading it—horrifying deficiencies in the translation.

The worst example of this happened once when Borges and I were in Oklahoma. We'd completed a day's work but instead of going for a walk, we decided to begin translating a new story he had finished dictating only the day before. As I had no rough draft of it, we translated from sight. The trouble with this is that I later felt committed to what Borges and I had put down on the page, and—inexplicably—I couldn't be free with it. Anyhow, the story was eventually bought by *Harper's,* and when they sent the galleys—this was four or five months after the translation was finished—I was scarlet with shame. I found the language so stilted I don't think there was a line I didn't change. The story had to be completely reset. It was "The Unworthy Friend." I'll never let this happen again, because I'll never allow us to do another sight translation.

QUESTION: Do you ever find mistranslations inspiring—in the sense that they might lead into a really interesting possibility?

DI GIOVANNI: Only to someone for whom the act of writing is a frivolity could a mistranslation seem interesting. If Borges wrote, "The sky is blue," and by slip or design I typed, "The sky is glue" and then thought the result greatly interesting, I should be a candidate for the madhouse. I'm still on the side of meaning in literature; I think too much gibberish is praised as "imaginative" and "poetic." Perhaps this is the fault of professors and pseudoscholars who look at writing through microscopes, placing too much emphasis on single words and abstractions and refusing to believe that writers write specifically about specific things.

Now, on another plane, the worst fault in a translation is not getting a word wrong but getting the author's tone, or voice, wrong. Mistranslations per se, when they don't show, are unimportant. Not, however, mistranslations like the "helmets–hoofs" business, which stops the reading and jerks you out of the poem. Borges' translations are crammed with this sort of thing, and in the work of a writer as precise and economical as he is, mistranslations are distortions. At the end of the story of Tadeo Isidoro Cruz, for example, there's a word, *"jinetas,"* which means "shoulder braid" or "insignia." In Spanish, there is also the word *"jinetes,"* which means "horsemen" or "riders." An earlier translator probably thought that, since the story had to do with horsemen, the word *"jinetas"* was a misprint. So instead of having the hero, who is about to take the side of the man he is hunting down, troubled over his rank and uniform—in other words, the emblems of his authority—the other translation has him troubled about "the other cavalrymen." Borges remarked that it was a wonder he hadn't taken *"jinetas"* for the feminine of *"jinetes"* and had the hero troubled about "the Amazons."

MAC SHANE: This seems a good example of the translator's losing sight of the general intention of the whole work.

DI GIOVANNI: Exactly. Borges' stories are so much sharper and more clearly detailed than most of the earlier translations show. I sometimes liken our work, when we make our own new translations, to cleaning a painting. We make the reader see things that aren't in the other versions. Here's another example, from the famous story "The Dead Man," in which the climax of the story occurs on New Year's Eve, the climax of the year. Borges wrote that "The closing scene of the story coincides with the commotion of the closing night of the year 1894." A sentence or two later, he speaks of the clock striking twelve. Perfect. That's what clocks do on New Year's Eve. But the other version reads, "The last scene of the drama corresponds to the upheaval of the last night." And later, "the bell tolls twelve." What last night? What bell? You see, the translator puts the reader in some dim no-man's-land, when what Borges is saying couldn't be clearer. I think one of the problems is that a lot of the early translators were intimidated by Borges' reputation for being deep. They equated being deep with being obscure, and they also associated Borges with dreams and a dreamlike, or vague, prose. Of course, I can see some professor

cont over

admiring the "tolling" of twelve o'clock as a clever foreshadowing of Otálora's death on the next page. But I assure you that Borges' intentions are lucid and definite—so much so that if sometimes I point out that a passage or a line seems obscure, he immediately volunteers to make the Spanish absolutely clear.

MAC SHANE: Does this mean there are new Spanish editions also coming out with these revisions?

DI GIOVANNI: I was speaking, really, of new work in manuscript, although we've caught a couple of things from the early stories and have been bringing out revised and corrected Spanish editions. One simple example of this occurred in "Ibn Hakkan al-Bokhari, Dead in His Labyrinth." Borges, at the story's close, wrote that the two characters met in a pub "three or four nights later," and farther along in the same paragraph one of them mentions their previous meeting "the night before last." This discrepancy was pointed out to us by the *New Yorker*'s editors, so we eagerly made the change in both English and Spanish to "two nights later." Of course, inevitably, a professor we know complained about Borges' tampering with his work; he considered the discrepancy charming and thought we should have left it alone. I asked him whether he'd been aware of it, and he said no. Borges was mildly angered; first of all, he found nothing charming in the slip, and, secondly, he feels he has the right to shape and alter his work as he sees fit. One of the great luxuries of working with Borges is that he's interested only in making things better and not in defending a text.

BORGES: No, God forbid!

DI GIOVANNI: I'm afraid a lot of other authors would prove very jealous of their originals.

BORGES: Of course, poetry is very mysterious. Take the lines from Shakespeare in which, speaking of Christ in Israel, he says:

> Over whose acres walk'd those blessed feet,
> Which, fourteen hundred years ago, were nail'd,
> For our advantage, on the bitter cross.

Now, I wonder whether the use of the word "advantage" for "salvation" was common in those days, or whether it was a personal gift of Shakespeare. It was the right word, yet a very unusual word —a word which, if translated, would be *"a la ventaja nuestra."* It is the right word, however, if properly and logically defended.

MAC SHANE: Isn't it the context that saves it?

BORGES: Of course, but there's also something unexplainable and mysterious. You feel "advantage" is the right word here—a word which in a sense is not very beautiful but sounds like the right word. And in the seventeenth century, "advantage" may have been used that way.

MAC SHANE: To mean "salvation"?

BORGES: Yes, by the theologians. So that in those days, perhaps, the line wasn't as beautiful as it is today. Nowadays, the word "advantage" comes with a sharp surprise. I am grateful to Shakespeare, but, for all we know, maybe time has bettered the text.

DI GIOVANNI: I'd like to close with an example of Borges' attitude toward his own text. One afternoon, when I was reading him a draft of the "Conjectural Poem," he stopped me to announce that the next phrase I was going to read—*"se ciernen sobre mí"*—he had imagined in English and translated into Spanish. He said his English line had been "loom over me." Undaunted, I read him my phrase, "tighten the ring around me." He didn't say, "Well, I'm sorry, it's 'loom over me'"; he told me to retain my words, which were more effective than his own.

BORGES: I thought "loom" a beautiful word—slow-sounding, slow-moving. Loom, loom, loom. But he was right.

Appendix
"The Writer's Apprenticeship"

"The Writer's Apprenticeship"
by Jorge Luis Borges

The poet's trade, the writer's trade, is a strange one. Chesterton said: "Only one thing is needful—everything." To a writer this everything is more than an encompassing word; it is literal. It stands for the chief, for the essential, human experiences. For example, a writer needs loneliness, and he gets his share of it. He needs love, and he gets shared and also unshared love. He needs friendship. In fact, he needs the universe. To be a writer is, in a sense, to be a day-dreamer—to be living a kind of double life.

I published my first book, *Fervor de Buenos Aires,* way back in 1923. This book was not in praise of Buenos Aires; rather, I tried to express the way I felt about my city. I know that I then stood in need of many things, for though at home I lived in a literary atmosphere—my father was a man of letters—still, that was not enough. I needed something more, which I eventually found in friendships and in literary conversation.

What a great university should give a young writer is precisely that: conversation, discussion, the art of agreeing, and, what is perhaps most important, the art of disagreeing. Out of all this, the moment may come when the young writer feels he can make his emotions into poetry. He should begin, of course, by imitating the writers he likes. This is the way the writer becomes himself through losing himself—that strange way of double living, of living in reality as much as one can and at the same time of living in that other reality, the one he has to create, the reality of his dreams.

This is the essential aim of the writing program at Columbia University's School of the Arts. I am speaking in behalf of the many young men and women at Columbia who are striving to be writers, who have not yet discovered the sound of their own voices. I have recently spent two weeks here, lecturing before eager student writers. I can see what these workshops mean to them; I can see how important they are for the advancement of literature. In my own land, no such opportunities are given young people.

Let us think of the still nameless poets, still nameless writers, who should be brought together and kept together. I am sure it is our duty to help these future benefactors to attain that final discovery of themselves which makes for great literature. Literature is not a mere juggling of words; what matters is what is left unsaid, or what may be read between the lines. Were it not for this deep inner feeling, literature would be no more than a game, and we all know that it can be much more than that.

We all have the pleasures of the reader, but the writer has also the pleasure and the task of writing. This is not only a strange but a rewarding experience. We owe all young writers the opportunity of getting together, of agreeing or disagreeing, and finally of achieving the craft of writing.

Index

Borges, Jorge Luis (cont.)
novel writing, 64; and Perón
regime, 60; and time, 7, 51, 57,
63, 64, 65; translations of his
work, 131–32, 157; works by,
"Aleph, The," 58; *Aleph and
Other Stories 1933–1969, The,*
5, 129, 136 (quoted); "Autobiographical Essay, An," 5–6
(quoted), 6–7 (quoted), 127–
30, 133; "Borges and Myself,"
96–97; "Circular Ruins, The,"
53, 118; "Congress, The," 64;
"Conjectural Poem," 119–20,
151–54, 152–54 (text), 160;
"Dead Man, The," 8 (quoted),
157–58; "Deathwatch on the
Southside," 138; "Deutsches Requiem," 60–61; *Doctor Brodie's
Report,* 5, 9 (quoted), 57, 64,
106; "Duel, The," 49–50, 106
(quoted); early essays, 130; early
verse, 71; "End of the Duel,
The," 10, 15–21 (text), 21–52,
53; *Fervor de Buenos Aires,* 71,
163; "Garden of Forking Paths,
The," 134 (quoted); "Gospel
According to Mark, The," 106;
"Hengest Cyning," 140; "Ibn
Hakkan al-Bokhari, Dead in His
Labyrinth," 158; *In Praise of
Darkness,* 145; "Invocation to
Joyce," 140–43, 141–43 (text);
"John I:14," 143–45, 143–45
(text); "Juan Muraña," 111;
"June 1968," 76–83, 77–78
(text), 91; "Keeper of the
Books, The," 83–91, 83–85
(text); "Life of Tadeo Isidoro

Cruz (1829–1874), The," 115–
127, 116–17 (quoted), 132,
156; "Meeting, The," 106;
"New Refutation of Time," 63,
64; "Page to Commemorate
Colonel Suárez, Victor at Junín,
A," 146–51, 146–47 (text, first
version), 149–51 (text, second
version); "Pedro Salvadores, 26
(quoted), 57–58 (quoted),
105–06; *Personal Anthology, A,*
146; "Pierre Menard, Author of
the *Quixote*," 54, 65; "Rosendo's Tale," 8 (quoted), 55, 111;
Selected Poems 1923–1967, 138–
41, 149; "South, The," 50;
"Streetcorner Man," 55–57, 113;
"Tlön, Uqbar, Orbis Tertius,"
53; translation of *The Wild
Palms,* 136; "Two Kings and
Their Two Labyrinths, The,"
109; *Universal History of Infamy, A,* 56, 113; "Unworthy
Friend, The," 111, 155;
"Watcher, The," 95–99, 95–96
(text)
Boswell, James, 58–59
Browne, Thomas, 6
Burton, Richard Francis, 109–10

Carroll, Lewis, 54
Chaucer, 104–05
Chesterton, G. K., 46, 55, 56, 62, 81,
163 (quoted)
"Children of Adam," 76
Chuang Tzu, 88, 90
Collins, Wilkie, 62
Columbia University writing pro-
gram, 9–11, 103, 164